MW00997811

FOXHUNTING ADVENTURES

THE DERRYDALE PRESS
FOXHUNTERS' LIBRARY

FOXHUNTING ADVENTURES

Chasing the Story

NORMAN FINE

Foreword by
James L. Young, ex-MFH

THE DERRYDALE PRESS
Lanham • New York • Plymouth, UK

THE DERRYDALE PRESS

Published by The Derrydale Press
An imprint of The Rowman & Littlefield Publishing Group, Inc.
4501 Forbes Boulevard, Suite 200, Lanham, Maryland 20706
http://www.rlpgtrade.com

Estover Road, Plymouth PL6 7PY, United Kingdom

Distributed by National Book Network and Millwood House, Ltd.,
www.foxhuntingadventures.com

Copyright © 2010 by Norman Fine

All rights reserved. No part of this book may be reproduced in any form or by any
electronic or mechanical means, including information storage and retrieval systems,
without written permission from the publisher, except by a reviewer who may quote
passages in a review.

British Library Cataloguing in Publication Information Available

Library of Congress Cataloging-in-Publication Data

Fine, Norman M.
Foxhunting adventures : chasing the story / Norman Fine.
p.   cm.
Includes bibliographical references and index.
ISBN 978-1-56416-212-0 (cloth : alk. paper)
1. Fox hunting—Anecdotes. I. Title.
SK285.F56 2010
799.2'59775—dc22
2010013602

∞™ The paper used in this publication meets the minimum requirements of American
National Standard for Information Sciences—Permanence of Paper for Printed Library
Materials, ANSI/NISO Z39.48-1992.

Printed in the United States of America

CONTENTS

ACKNOWLEDGMENTS

I wish to thank the "team" of friends who helped me with this book.

First-Friend is my wife, Joan, who is my sounding board and reliable dispenser of good judgment. Although she is my toughest editor, she is at the same time my heartiest supporter—always—in every venture. Joan was partner and witness to all of the early hunting adventures described here, and when she contracted the incurable retriever field trial bug I was sorry to lose her from the hunting field.

James L. Young has made enormous contributions to the sport of foxhunting as MFH of the renowned Orange County Hunt in Virginia, as a director and ultimately president of the Masters of Foxhounds Association, as president of the Virginia Foxhound Club, and as a member of the Advisory Board of the Museum of Hounds and Hunting. I am deeply honored that Jimmy agreed to write the foreword to this book.

If I possess one talent, it's recognizing a good idea when I hear it. Author-editor Steven Price in New York City has long been my secret weapon of creative ideas. Steve read every story, did a first-pass copy edit, and, true to form, dispensed valuable and welcome ideas.

Jed Lyons, president of the Rowman & Littlefield Publishing Group, is another friend who deserves not only my thanks but the thanks of all foxhunters. By maintaining The Derrydale Press imprint—probably the smallest and certainly the least profitable of all Rowman & Littlefield imprints—he is keeping alive the most illustrious publishing name in North American foxhunting literature.

I have long admired the work of Piper Wallis, Director of Design at Rowman & Littlefield, and I was thrilled to learn that she would personally create the cover design for this book.

In the time I have been associated with Rowman & Littlefield, Stephen Driver has risen from Assistant Editor to Vice President of Production Services. He is an efficient project manager and a pleasure to work with. Once a completed package is in Stephen's hands, I relax in the knowledge that all details will be handled, and the schedule will be met.

I rely on foxhunter Anne Moe from Maryland any time I need a copy-editor. She polished *Covertside* magazine for me for years. How anyone can know which compound words should be hyphenated, which should not, which should be put together as one word, and which should be separated into two words, I cannot begin to imagine.

I am sincerely grateful to those talented photographers—all of whom I have worked with on other projects—who generously allowed me to reproduce their images. What is a book on foxhunting without a Jim Meads photo? There are four of them here. There are two photos each from Jim Duggan, who captured an amazing shot of coyote and hounds; from Noel Mullins, a talented writer and photographer from Ireland; and from Garth Thompson, whose brilliant images of African wildlife have been published around the world. Other photographs are reproduced through the courtesy of Bella Vita Fotografie, Jake Carle, Evelyn C. Cowles, Susan Edwards, Martin Engel, Catherine French, William Gamble, Gamecock, Karen L. Myers, Ray Orth, David Pollock, Curtis Robb, Kathy Tourney, and Debbie Turner. Finally, a personal tribute to the late Akhtar Hussein, whose scenic photograph of the white cliffs bordering War Eagle Creek in the Arkansas Ozarks is included here. The artistry of this distinguished feature photographer was internationally recognized, and the sport of foxhunting was fortunate to have fired his imagination and lured him to the field.

FOREWORD

Fresh from fifteen years as founder and editor of the award-winning *Covertside* magazine, Norman Fine has produced this marvelous collection of foxhunting memories from his experiences both at home and abroad. The fact that his formal training as an engineer in no way hinders his poetic muse from expressing herself herein provides worthy grounds for investment in this treasure trove of delightful sporting reminiscences. The man's writings fairly capture the reader and take him headlong o'er the fences and the hedges of hunts from North America to the old sod of Ireland and England.

But hunting recitations, per se, do not produce elevated sports writing such as Fine's. His sporting diary paints larger-than-life characters in human, equine, and canine forms. There is the "black, hairy beast," of which Norm is warned: "Don't argue with him." There are uncommon obstacles, one of which is actually negotiated by the use of a horse's elbows!

Where Norman's practical skills become a boon to his narrative is in the overarching depth and breadth of his particulars. You want historical context? It is woven into the tale. You fancy the pedigree history of famous hounds? He provides it as readable fabric of the anecdote. Lively characters a necessity? They're part of the woof and warp of the true accounts.

I will sorely miss Norman Fine's singular touch in the new *Covertside* magazine, while wishing the new editor a genuine "Good Luck!" This marvelous book, however, softens the loss and bodes well for future offerings from Norm. I have no doubt that any and all of his work will stand equally beside those of Beckford, Surtees, Higginson, and Mackay-Smith.

James L. Young, ex-MFH
Marshall, Virginia
March 2010

INTRODUCTION

Books about foxhunting are generally written by a celebrated huntsman, a brilliant hound breeder, an illustrious Master of Foxhounds. I'm none of these.

What, then, emboldens me to write a book about foxhunting?

I am a student, an observer, a chronicler, a reporter who has hunted with more than fifty different hunts around the world for over forty years. More recently, as creator and editor for fifteen years of *Covertside*—the only foxhunting magazine in North America—and as editor for ten years of The Derrydale Press Foxhunters' Library, I had an unparalleled opportunity to visit, to ride behind, to interview, to observe many of the greatest huntsmen, hound breeders, and Masters of Foxhounds of the last half-century.

My introduction to foxhunting was with the Nashoba Valley Hunt in Massachusetts shortly after it was established. The huntsman was an unforgettable Irishman—Mike Murphy—who could snap a cigarette from the lips of a smoker with his hunt whip. He demonstrated his skill one day with the cooperation of my then girlfriend, now wife of forty-two years, Joan, who has never been known—before or since—to back down from a challenge. At about the same time, my friend and stable owner Nick Rodday organized the first of many foxhunting trips to Ireland. It was there that I caught the contagious mad-keen-Irish foxhunting bug that changed my life.

Joan and I were among the first hunting guests to book into Scarteen, home of the late Thady Ryan, MFH, and his lovely wife, Anne.

Scarteen was also home to the famed "Black and Tans"—hounds owned and bred by the Ryan family for three hundred years. And what voices! When the Scarteen hounds were in full cry a field ahead, it resonated for all the world as if you were enclosed with them inside a large wooden barrel.

A world-class huntsman and an Irish national treasure renowned throughout the sporting world, Thady was nevertheless an incredibly modest man and a patient teacher. After a day's hunting, back at Scarteen and with a twinkle in his eye, he would freely admit to all his missed opportunities of the day.

"Did you see when Generous took that line down the *bohreen* and the rest of the pack went over the bank? I should have trusted her!" he would say, and then proceed to describe the intricacies of the chase as it unfolded. Those debriefing sessions with Thady fired my curiosity to learn more.

With the Massachusetts foxhunting season ending each year when the ground froze—usually the end of November or early December— Joan and I began to visit Virginia to extend our season. There I had the great good fortune to meet the late Alexander Mackay-Smith, who was to become one of my dearest friends through the last twelve years of his life.

A man of enormous intellect, Alex merged sport, literature, art, music, and the humanities seamlessly. With twelve books to his credit, he was the most prolific author of equine sporting scholarship in North America. He was editor of the *Chronicle of the Horse* for almost twenty-five years. He was a founder of numerous sporting institutions, among them the United States Pony Clubs, the United States Combined Training Association, the National Sporting Library, and the American Academy of Equine Artists.

Alex became a mentor to me on foxhunting history and sporting literature. Through him I was to get to know other luminaries of America's foxhunting firmament, including James L. Young, MFH of the famed Orange County Hunt and passionate devotee of sporting literature and history. It was to Alex that I first broached the idea for a foxhunting newsletter, later magazine—*Covertside*—to be published by the MFHA. Alex liked the idea and suggested that I talk to Jimmy Young, then president of the association. With the further support of the previous president, C. Martin Wood III, MFH, who agreed to fund the new venture from the MFHA Educational Foundation, *Covertside* was whelped.

As editor of both *Covertside* and The Derrydale Press Foxhunters' Library, my foxhunting acuity was further shaped by talking hounds and hunting on many occasions with the late Ronnie Wallace when MFH of the Exmoor in England; Hugh Robards, former huntsman of the Limerick in Ireland, when he became MFH and huntsman of the Rolling Rock in the United States; Ben Hardaway, MFH of the Midland; Marty Wood, MFH of the Live Oak; the Poe brothers— Melvin, huntsman of the Orange County, and Albert, huntsman of the Piedmont and the Middleburg; and scores of younger and des- tined-for-fame Masters and huntsmen of today.

I have been fascinated not only by the sport and the science of hunting with hounds but with the widely disparate cultures and per- sonalities that render each hunt unique and worthy of observation and recording. I hope these stories will convey that fascination. I have tried to connect them in a way that describes my journey from a rider of horses to an observant "foxhunting man." That journey was a learning process that started with the horse, carried me into all manner of hunting cultures and countries, and finally to the beginnings of an awareness of the art and science of venery.

I say "the beginnings of an awareness" because there is no end to the learning process. The subject of foxhunting embraces a complex four-way relationship among four different living creatures—ourselves, our horses, our hounds, and the quarry—with lines of communication running and crisscrossing among all four parties. Add to that the inan- imate variables of terrain, weather, and scent, and you have a subject worthy of a lifetime of study.

Even a minimal amount of study, though, will pay dividends. I urge all new foxhunters to read a good book and pay just a little more attention to what is happening both in the field and in the kennels. Read about the practices and philosophies of the great hound breeders and huntsmen; observe and appreciate the highly sophisticated relationship between huntsman and hound; pick up on the clues revealed by the body language of the hunting hound; witness the drama of the ancient conflict between hunter and hunted, a conflict to which every extant creature owes its existence. By so doing you will immeasurably enhance your own enjoyment of every hunting day.

There are many excellent books that will help you along this journey of discovery. I've provided a reading list at the end. Try some of them. You won't be sorry!

Norman Fine
Millwood, Virginia
January 2010

FOXHUNTING ADVENTURES

1

ANY REASONABLE HORSE

Ireland, 1973

Since I came to foxhunting through a love of horses, it's not surprising that my earliest hunting tales focused more on horses than on hounds. One night during a dinner party at home, I related the following experience to our guests. After the telling, I realized this was more than just a horse story. It was a glimpse into the capacity of an animal whose physical potential and inborn generosity most of us scarcely even begin to call upon.

When the nights turn crisp and the dinner talk turns to tales of fox-hunting, I like to share a bit of philosophy imparted to me by that special animal—part horse, part cat, and all heart—the Irish hunter. That remarkable creature understands something of the flavor of life. He never allows natural caution, reticence, or conservatism to limit his perception of the possible.

The Scarteen hounds were hunting a most unusual piece of country in Kilcommon, County Limerick, this day. A wild and forbidding landscape, far from the well-traveled roads, high into the hills, it was unknown country even to Master Thady Ryan. To complete the scene, a dense fog obliterated every feature of the landscape.

Hounds found in the very first covert. The field galloped forward blindly through the thick, hanging mist in a tight pack. To delay was to be left alone and disoriented. Disdaining the crowd, however, my new English friend Richard swung his horse away. With an ear to the chorusing hounds, he chose his own line, and I followed.

Thady Ryan, MFH, with his devoted whipper-in, Tommy O'Dwyer, and the Scarteen hounds, from an oil painting by Peter Curling. A print of this painting hangs above the fireplace in my library. On the occasion of Thady's 1995 trip to the United States to judge the Virginia Foxhound Show, he and Anne came for dinner. Over drinks he spied the painting. "Did you dig that out of the closet and knock the dust off just for my visit?" he asked. "No, Thady," I replied. "It lives there."

Enveloped in a gray, colorless sphere of our own with no more than fifty feet of visibility in any direction, we two galloped over this no man's land. We soon lost all sound of hounds, horn, or humanity. On we cantered in what direction one couldn't possibly know. I wondered if we would ever again see another living soul.

Finally, far off, barely audible through the moist air, the horn reached us. We set off in the direction of that welcome sound, but were soon brought up short by a most formidable obstacle.

Before us was a sliding bank leading down to the narrow shore of a swiftly moving stream. Although the stream seemed jumpable, the opposite shore offered only two feet of width before meeting the sheer face of a high vertical bank.

In amazement, I watched Richard point his horse down the slide with the casual confidence of a man descending the front steps of his house. He reached the bottom, jumped the stream, and there his journey ended. The scant two-foot shoreline forced his horse to turn parallel to the vertical bank, and he was trapped. It was perfectly clear to me that the whole maneuver was impossible.

Richard was unfazed by his predicament. Although he couldn't even see over the cliff beside him, he swung his horse's head toward it time and time again, kicking, swatting, and cursing the horse's cowardice. His color and his voice rose precipitously. He turned to me as I sat transfixed by the futility of his efforts and shouted, "Come down and give us a lead over. I don't know what's got into this horse of mine."

Staring dumbly into his red face, astonished by his expectations, and thoroughly intimidated by the combination of obstacles before me, I could think only to appeal to whatever shred of judgment he might possess. I asked quietly, "Is it possible for a horse to do that?"

Achieving yet another shade of crimson, Richard turned his horse to the bank once again and shouted, punctuating each word with a kick and a swat.

"Any . . . *reasonable* . . . horse . . . can . . . do . . . this!"

Several kicks and swats later, exhausted by his efforts, he gave up on his horse as unreasonable.

Somehow those words had a magical effect upon me. Uttered as they were with absolute conviction, I believed him. I closed my legs and pointed my horse down the slide. He slid down on his hocks. As we reached the near shore, I asked him to jump the stream. He leaped toward the narrow shore opposite and the high facing bank. My only hope was to keep him straight. I separated both my hands so he couldn't turn. His front feet touched. As his hind feet hit the shore I closed my legs, clucked, and grabbed the mane to free his head. He thrust off his hocks.

Time stopped. In slow motion I saw a sight that I never again expect to see in a lifetime of riding. As I stared straight ahead into the vertical bank, his two front feet rose into view before my face. His hooves continued their miraculous journey upward until he had hooked his elbows on top of the bank. Inch by inch on his elbows, his hind feet scrambling for purchase against the vertical wall, we progressed upward. Time resumed. We were standing on top.

"Well done!" shouted my English friend. I heard several kicks and thumps from below, and a moment later Richard and his horse stood beside me. We trotted off in the direction of the horn—two unreasonable men on two reasonable horses.

2

THE BUNRATTEN FOX

Ireland, 1972

In addition to our time at Scarteen in County Limerick, Joan and I would stay for a week or so in County Galway at the home of the late Lady Molly Cusack-Smith, MFH, and huntsman of the Bermingham and North Galway hounds.

Bermingham House was a large Georgian mansion filled with furnishings of the period, Georgian silver, and floor-length velvet window drapes as thick as horse blankets. The splendor, however, had faded sometime in the previous century. Drapery hems had loosened, and plaster was falling. In short, it was a real Irish country estate of a time before the Common Market and prosperity.

As I recall, the first thing that we would do after being shown to our usual room was to throw back the bed sheets and sweep out the mouse droppings. We knew from experience that they would not be improved by the bed-warming pan slipped between the sheets by the housekeeper later in the evening.

This is the first story I ever sold for publication. It's a true ghost story. It also earned me the most money I was ever paid for a story in my thirty years of scribbling since. Perhaps that's one reason why CLASSIC magazine, as lovely as it was, went out of business.

"Nothing ever happens in the *Wesht* of Ireland."

That's what Sean O'Connell used to say, with his crooked smile and an odd glint in his eye. There seemed to be a message he was inviting me to read. That much I could see at the time, but no more.

Now as I look back with improved visibility, I begin to see behind his eyes the faintest reflections of a private, secret world that has no place in this day and age. But then, the West of Ireland does not pretend to notice this day and age.

As I cast back to reconstruct the events, I shall chronicle—changing only a few names—what I saw as well as memory serves.

My wife, Joan, and I arrive at Shannon Airport and pass through customs smoothly. A friendly agent unzips our saddle cases and pumps a few perfunctory sprays of disinfectant onto the saddle pads, more a symbolic gesture than an effective fumigation, we are sure.

A smiling man greets us waving a pair of car keys. "I didn't know when you were arriving, so I've been here and back twice already this morning." Although we have not changed our flight plans or itinerary, I apologize to Mr. Foley for wasting so much of his time trying to deliver our rental car to us.

"Time? (a wave of the hand) No matter; not to worry." And he cheerfully leads us at a brisk pace to the car.

Driving north, the countryside begins to sprout the graceful stone walls that delight the photographer and excite the foxhunter. Unlike the solid stone walls of our native New England, these are built precariously, one stone upon the other, only one stone in thickness. Up to five feet in height, they meander airily over the fields, defying gravity. If part of a wall does topple on occasion, it is patiently rebuilt.

A few hours later, in the village of Tuam, near Galway, we turn into the long drive that carries us to the great front doors of Bermingham House. This eighteenth-century Georgian mansion has been the family home of our hostess, Lady Molly Cusack-Smith (still known in town as Molly O'Rourke), since grander days when it was more easily maintained.

Lady Molly is a direct descendant of John Denis, one of Ireland's legendary horsemen. The first Master and huntsman of the Galway Blazers early in the nineteenth century, tales of Denis's skill with foxhounds and daring over steeplechase hurdles and hunt race fences are still recounted with awe throughout the pubs and parlors of County Galway.

The author (left) and an American friend, Steve Allen, mount up in the stable yard at Berming-ham House, 1969. *Joan Fine photo*

In Denis's later years, when competitors' complaints reached him concerning an impossible course of obstacles he had designed for a hunt race, he reacted characteristically. Pulling his horse from the field, he leaped aboard and galloped over the entire course—without saddle or bridle.

Today, fit and vigorous in her middle fifties, Lady Molly hunts her own pack, the Bermingham and North Galway hounds, in Galway's stone wall country. A powerful personality, commanding and stat-uesque, she is one of those rare individuals who make an instant impact and leave a permanent imprint.

Mixed with the joy of returning to Ireland is some bad news Joan and I learn upon our arrival at Bermingham House. Lady Molly's beloved friend, Sean O'Connell, was killed in an automobile accident several months ago.

My mind floods with images of this captivating young man, the wandering ninth Earl of Dartmoor, who in one short year had won the admiration and affection of Molly's household. I see him in this very parlor, delighting Molly and her guests with his easy banter. His warm and relaxed manner is kept in constant check by the faintest mocking twist of his voice. We had met just a year ago, shortly after he and his wife had arrived from Africa. They had bought the long-abandoned Bunratten estate in Molly's hunting country and were busily engaged in clearing the tangled land for farming.

Images of Sean in the hunt field flash through the mind: his lean frame carrying his well-worn hunt attire with aristocratic ease; his first hunt with Molly exactly one year ago today; me galloping behind him, engraving in my memory his flamboyant style over the walls. I see Sean O'Connell captured as in a colored plate of an antique sporting book, leaning back as his horse soars, one arm stretched to the sky, the tails of his scarlet hunt coat streaming behind, hard pressed to keep up. His love for the fox, keenness for the chase, and reckless abandon for following any line taken by hounds amplified the adventure we all felt.

Some months later, Molly had offered and Sean had accepted the Joint-Mastership of her pack. He shared this honor with one other gentleman, Sherman Russell, a warm, sentimental American who grew to love him as well.

But now Sean is gone. I tug my thoughts back to the present, where the discussion in Molly's parlor has shifted to tomorrow's hunt. Oddly, Molly has decided not to participate, but to allow her able first whipper-in, Michael Dempsey, to hunt her hounds instead. At this moment I cannot know how swiftly the accepted realities of my jet age are receding.

Molly surveys her guests with a smiling but measuring air and leads the way into the dining room. She swiftly directs the seating arrangements, and Joan is pleased to take her place at Molly's right.

If any room can be considered the heart of Bermingham House, it is this one. The instant impressions are fireglow, rich mahogany, and old silver. The room is heated by the great fireplace and illuminated by a profusion of candlelight. The huge table and sideboard have held forth in their present locations for more than a hundred years. Time-worn, burnished Georgian silverware, magnificent candelabra, and spectacular hunt race trophies bearing their inscriptions like a history of Irish sport reflect the firelight, warm it, age it, and finally pass it on to enrich the dark mahogany.

Dominating the end wall above the sideboard and presiding in spirit equal to Molly's presence, gray-whiskered John Denis surveys all from the saddle. This breathcatching nineteenth-century portrait of man, horse, and hound in a graceful swirl of motion and muscle was presented to him by grateful members of the Galway field.

After an elegant dinner, we return to the parlor for a final drink. With a hunting morning to follow, the fire is no longer fed, and the night chill quickly invades the retreating glow. Joan remains flushed, partly due to the dinner, wine, and conversation, but mainly, I think, because of the long johns concealed under her floor-length skirt.

Sherman Russell hands me a brandy, clutches his own with satisfaction, and lowers himself into a comfortable chair with a broad smile and a deep sigh. Russell's dependable attitude of well-being spreads like an umbrella, embracing all who are near. His conversation explodes with enthusiasm. A bachelor in his middle years, he has arranged his life thoughtfully to accommodate his one great passion—Irish foxhunting. Each November brings him from his Massachusetts home to Ireland and Bermingham House, where he is welcomed warmly by everyone from pubkeeper to chambermaid. Until the season ends in March, he is a part of Ireland as few Americans can ever be. With a love for this charmed land as honest and pure as his heart, he shares with the Irish those mystical journeys between reality and fantasy without questioning the boundaries. Turning to Molly, Russell again tries to persuade her to hunt her hounds the next day, but she remains firm.

"Michael will do perfectly well with my darlings." She is silent a moment. "But he does terribly like to kill fox. Just like Fanshawe at the Blazers. All they want to do is kill fox." Absorbed and withdrawn,

Molly contemplates her guests then turns to me. "You shall hunt Moose tomorrow."

I try to look pleased, but my mind is less so. Why me, and why that horse? Her favorite, Moose is a monstrous, black, hairy beast with feet like dinner plates. Although Mollie ascribes to him the greatest powers and purest virtues, I cannot dismiss the many stories of former passengers left lying in an Irish field as Moose and the hunt gallop on.

"Moose is a fairy, you know," says Molly. "Not really a horse at all. He insists upon hunting tomorrow even though I shan't. Good night and God bless."

Morning dawns slowly in the Irish winter. It is gray and cold. We eat our breakfast standing, backsides to the fireplace for warmth. Ignoring the chill, Michael Dempsey gulps his coffee by the door, impatient at the rare prospect of hunting hounds himself.

Arriving at the pub fixed for the meet, we find the usual commotion. Horses, vanned loose in Ireland, are being unboxed and tacked up. Friends greet one another enthusiastically. Trailers and vans continue to arrive.

Since hounds have not yet appeared, Joan and I head for the pub. At the bar Molly is conversing with two farmers in tweed caps and gum boots. Although I haven't adopted the Irish custom of drinking before the meet, I spy Molly's old groom, Will, and offer him a drink. His nut-brown face lights up. "I will. A small Irish."

Outside, hounds are arriving. Molly moves to the door, watches me approach Moose, and wishes me a good day with the horse. Stopping momentarily, she adds, "Don't argue with him."

Hounds, fresh and eager, are packed in tightly around Dempsey's horse as he stops to receive the inevitable final instructions from Molly. She seems tense and preoccupied, but so am I. I take hold of Moose's reins, mane, and saddle, and Will gives me a leg up . . . and up.

A handsome woman aboard an elegant hunter turns to me with

genuine delight. "You have Moose, have you? How wonderful! Just don't pick a fight with him!"

As we trot toward the first covert, Moose's powerful hindquarters pumping underneath me, his great feet clattering on the pavement, I resolve to be as tactful as possible.

The hunt begins slowly, with hounds moving an unimaginative fox to and fro within a relatively small thicket, keeping the action to a minimum. Dempsey finally picks up hounds, and we all follow at a brisk trot to another covert. Moose seems to have accepted me, and I begin to relax somewhat.

Russell, usually ebullient when hunting, checks his horse and soberly comes to a halt. As I pull up alongside, he leans over and informs me that we have just crossed the spot on the road where Sean O'Connell was killed.

There is a sudden explosion, signaled first by the excited cry of hounds and reaffirmed by the stirring staccato of Dempsey's horn signaling the *Gone Away*. The fox has broken covert and is flying. Hounds are following steadily, their voices chorusing the excitement. As I gallop in pursuit, I can hear snatches of conversation, shredded by the wind, between Dempsey and Russell far up front.

". . . fool of a fox . . . running straight upwind . . . why would he . . . ?"

". . . heading for Bunratten. . . ."

A field away, the fox gains a low stone wall and flies it in stride, his red brush streaming behind. Another image engraved in memory. The back of my neck prickles even now in recollection.

Moose is fulfilling Molly's promise. His earthshaking stride has lengthened to flowing grace. All the segments of his immense bulk have coordinated themselves, leaving the earth below us and reality behind. Small fields separated by stone walls stretch endlessly ahead as I succumb to his rhythm. I am a passenger. Each lacy wall floats toward me before disappearing below as Moose flies it and gallops on, the soft green carpet muting the beat of his hooves.

In the distance, the dark grove of Bunratten, once more abandoned, takes form. O'Connell's work had not progressed greatly against the long-neglected growth of tree, vine, and bush.

In his unnatural course straight into the wind, the fox's scent smacks the hounds full in the face. They need no pause as they press at top speed. Disdaining wile and cunning, the reckless fox maintains his long dash for Bunratten, reaches his goal, and plunges into the thickets of the empty estate.

Now within the darkness of the woods, he resorts to seemingly supernatural evasions. His elusive tactics confuse the hounds, who cross their own tracks and cross them again. A full hour passes. He is viewed many times. The muffled *holloas* are heard first from one end of the plantation, then the other. But when hounds arrive he is gone.

A fanatical determination has settled into Michael Dempsey's rigid face. He encourages his hounds. They strain in concentration, their noses sampling every scrap of earth, every leaf and twig for the faintest trace of lingering scent. Again an excited *find* declared by the short, plaintive cry of a hardworking hound. But nothing. The fox is like a ghost.

"Leave it, Michael," Russell pleads. But Dempsey must have his day.

A second hour passes. Urged by Dempsey, hounds press on. Still the fox refuses to leave Bunratten. He is viewed again, coat matted, brush weighted with fatigue. When the last of his endurance ebbs, the contest must end.

It finally happens. A brief scuffle is heard in the deepest covert. Dempsey leaps to the ground, ducks into the brush, and a few moments later his horn mournfully signals the kill.

I look at Sherman Russell. He is white and shaken. The woods are suddenly still. The Irish say nothing, but their eyes trade the unspoken secret, one to the other. With tears trickling down his weathered cheeks, Russell slowly unscrews his flask, takes a gulp of brandy, and pours the rest onto the scarred ground for Sean.

3

THE DAY I WHIPPED-IN

1986

One day in early December 1983, I found myself hacking back to the Nashoba Valley Hunt meet in the company of friends after the last hunt of our Massachusetts season. It had ended all too soon, and at that precise, morose moment I decided to continue my season elsewhere.

"I'm going to Virginia," I announced. "If anyone wants to come with me, let me know."

I received a solitary reply. "I'll come with you," said my friend Herb Richman.

Herb and I—Joan was a new associate at a Boston law firm at the time and "billable hours" was her mantra—booked into the Hunting Box in Boyce, Virginia. Proprietors Cliff and Laura Hunt catered to visiting fox-hunters, providing beds, meals, hirelings, and transport to at least ten Virginia hunts not more than an hour's drive away.

Being the dutiful husband I am, I called Joan every evening (at her office) to give her a recap of my hunting day. Stupidly, I hadn't a clue that every phone call was adding coals to a smoldering fire of envy. Mercifully, instead of unloading her mounting frustrations upon me, she took a more practical approach. On my next evening's call, I was instructed as to the arrival time of the flight she had booked for the following day.

Thus began our annual holiday and vacation trips to the Hunting Box, which became more and more frequent until we finally decided to turn our lives upside-down and move permanently to Virginia, a decision we have never regretted.

I knew all about whipping-in. I had read Peter Beckford's treatise, *Thoughts on Hunting*. True, I hadn't actually done it. But I had been a member of the field for twenty years in my native Massachusetts. So I leaped with enthusiasm and confidence to accept the invitation of my Virginia host, Cliff Hunt, honorary whipper-in to the Blue Ridge hounds, to accompany him in his sporting duties that morning.

What Beckford hadn't revealed through his pages, as I was to find out that day, was the pounding mileage, the face-raking branches, the climbing down and the climbing up, the knee-smashing and ankle-twisting trees, the constant motion, the numbing exhaustion. Would I trade that day for the rest of my season? No way. That was the day I discovered what I had been missing for twenty years.

I climbed aboard Uno, the young chestnut Thoroughbred that Cliff had brought for me, and followed my leader to the hound truck. Out poured a river of hounds. They milled exuberantly about huntsman Chris Howells, MFH Judith Greenhalgh, and first whipper-in Bobby Joe Pillion. The field, which included my wife, Joan, and several hunting friends from New England, was clustered dutifully behind Field Master Joan Batterton, standing well apart from us. I experienced a vague feeling of discomfort—as if I were out of place. That's what Twenty Years in the Field do to you, I guess.

Hounds moved off and so did Cliff. I trotted close behind on Uno. We veered away from the pack, trotted the length of the wooded covert, and turned into a trail bordering the far end of the wood. We stopped after about fifty yards.

"Stay here and make some noise," Cliff said. "Chris is drawing through and we don't want the fox coming out this side. We can't get through the country in that direction." With those instructions he trotted off.

Make some noise? For Twenty Years in the Field I'd been conditioned to be silent. This was indeed going to be a different kind of day. Make some noise? I slapped my hunt whip against my boot. As a result of my previous conditioning the first few tentative slaps sounded like explosions in the silent wood.

Gradually I warmed up to my job. "Hey guy, hey guy, chip, chip, chip," I uttered. No wrathful Field Master descended on me. No one excused me from the field. I was quite alone and I was supposed to make noise! Slap, slap went my whip with enthusiasm.

"Hey guy, hey guy," I yodeled into the wooded thicket in my best huntsman's voice. I kept this up for perhaps five or ten minutes, seeing nothing and hearing nothing until Cliff came trotting back.

"Chris is out the other side," he said. "Let's move on." At once he was away at the canter, me in his wake. We broke out of the woods, crossed a large field, and came to a farm gate where we were forced to stop. Cliff slid off his horse, opened the gate, and let us through.

"I'll just lead my horse across this field instead of remounting," he said. "There's a gate on the other side that has to be opened as well."

Thus I gained the vantage point for my first moment of glory. Cliff walked and I rode across the field, which rose to a gentle knoll. Uno and I reached the crest ahead of Cliff. From there the ground fell away gradually to the fence line along a hedgerow. The gate Cliff had spoken of was set in the corner.

As I stood waiting for Cliff to catch up, a fresh red fox slipped out of the covert, loped across the corner of the field, ducked under the gate, and went away along the far side of the hedgerow. I turned to Cliff who was trudging up the hill and said excitedly, *"Tally-ho!"* That brought him to life. Dragging his horse behind him, he trotted the rest of the way up the hill and *holloaed* for Chris.

Chris's horn answered, sending his hounds on to the *holloa*, and in a very few moments Chris was topping the knoll with the pack.

Cliff and Laura Hunt (left) operated the Hunting Box in Boyce, Virginia. They provided lodging, meals, and hirelings to visiting foxhunters. Many of their clientele became Virginia residents after first experiencing the local brand of foxhunting from the Hunts' establishment. In this 1980s photo, Joan is on Elba, a 16.2-hand Thoroughbred–Quarter Horse cross who

jumped anything she was pointed at and hunted well into her twenties. I am on Saint Nicholas, a Thoroughbred cross I hunted from the age of five until he was twenty. Both horses we first hired, then purchased from Cliff Hunt.

Hounds tumbled down the hill, swarming along both sides of the hedgerow. A joyous yelp came from the far side. The find was affirmed by another and yet another, and presently the pack was away on fine terms with their fox. Inwardly I patted myself on the back.

AFTER THE PACK

Cliff mounted quickly, and we were off at a gallop in the wake of the hounds. The pack swung somewhat left-handed, but Cliff headed to the right, angling toward the Shenandoah River. Looking behind I saw the field and my friends just cresting the knoll where the fox had been viewed away and hounds put on to follow. That was all minutes ago and past. This is where the action is, I exulted, and careened down the lane after Cliff.

The lane ended and we turned left onto a wide cinder road that ran alongside the river to our right. On our left was a wire fence separating us from the narrow, flat floodplain that wound along the course of the river. Bordering the far side of the floodplain was a tree-covered ridge also following the river course. Hounds were screaming their way through the trees along the ridge.

I pounded on after Cliff, who continued at a full gallop down the cinder road, his ear cocked to the ridge. He looked increasingly worried. Ahead in the distance I could see an end to this so far endless road. There appeared to be an embankment way off and I suddenly understood the concern on Cliff's face. We were headed straight for U.S. Route 50 where it crossed the river, a major east–west highway with four lanes of divided traffic at that point.

Cliff turned to shout to me. Between snatches of hound music reaching us from the ridge, the wind in my ears and the pelting of cinders from Cliff's horse's flying feet, I managed to hear at least some of what he shouted. ". . . have to whip them off . . . before . . . cross Route 50."

Nearing the embankment the aspect of the countryside changed dramatically. We drew our lathered horses up. The green river valley fields ended. The fence line by the road ended and turned left toward the ridge. From this point for perhaps fifty yards to the highway embankment grew a dense tangle of wooded thicket and hanging vines.

The gloomy interior had been rendered surreal by the retreat of the high floodwaters two months earlier that had left grass and debris clinging to branches and vines to a height well over our heads. Cliff plunged into the thicket to head off the oncoming hounds. Uno and I bushwhacked through in pursuit, at the same time trying to preserve my kneecaps. The vines and branches, draped thickly with hanging grass and other detritus of the flood, shut out the sky above us as in some prehistoric forest.

MFH Greenhalgh and her guest, Shirley Morgan, MFH, had somehow penetrated the wood ahead of us. The four of us spread out as the first hounds appeared. Crack, went Cliff's whip. "Hark to him; Hark to him! Get back there," he shouted, crashing about to head off one hound then another. "Stop that hound!" he shouted to me.

I wheeled Uno around and managed to get ahead of a hard-working hound, nose to the ground. I had never, never, actually cracked my whip at a hound. I gave a tentative snap. "Hark to him," I bleated.

Behind me I heard the unmistakable rumble of the eighteen-wheelers on Route 50. My inhibitions fled. *Crack* went my whip. "Hark to him! Get your head up!" I yelled. The hound turned back.

My elation was short-lived. Two more hounds, noses to the ground, were trying to hunt through. I crashed my way over ahead of the pair. "Hark to him! Get back! Hark to him!" *Crack!* They looked up and trotted back uncertainly.

The woods on both sides of me rang out with whip-cracks and shouts. The four of us raced back and forth stopping hounds and hoping Chris would show up soon to call them in. One hound would slip through every now and again, but our efforts were definitely prevailing.

Finally, above the noise of the shouts, whips, and tearing brush and vines, we heard Chris's horn. We had stopped them and turned them, and he was calling them in.

We made our way back out to the cinder road. The field had arrived in time to see Chris calling hounds to him. I lamented inwardly for my friends. The excitement was over. Is this what I'd been missing for Twenty Years in the Field?

OFF AGAIN

We had a long trot back to the next covert that Chris intended to draw. Again Cliff galloped off. I followed. Looking behind I saw the field stopped and waiting. I couldn't begin to figure how many more miles we were putting in by comparison. It seemed we were always moving.

Hark! Hounds were speaking again. They were working a fox through a large covert in front of us. Cliff and I moved slowly ahead posting ourselves in good position to view, should the fox break out on our side.

We saw nothing, but hounds were still working and speaking. Cliff decided to retrace our steps. We jumped over a coop off the road, cantered across a small field, and entered a patch of woods where we ran smack into the field. "Staff, please," someone barked, and Twenty Years in the Field conditioning had me ready to pull up and look for a place off the trail to back into, when I realized the "Staff, please" was for me. Horses and riders scattered off the trail as we claimed our "right of way." I grinned at my friends shamelessly as we cantered through.

The hound music became more urgent. We emerged into a large field as Chris and the hounds burst from the covert. The lead hounds were yelping with excitement as they scrambled into the field, overran the line, and checked. I stood there in the midst of the oncoming pack and watched, entranced, as the lead hounds cast themselves in a perfect circle about me. I had never been this close to the drama.

The pack continued their cast, enlarging the circle. One hound hit the line and spoke. The circle collapsed as the other hounds rushed to him. Another hound hit it, then another, and they were off again in full cry.

I found myself galloping beside Chris as we raced out into another large field. The pack was bunched directly in front of us, running straight and screaming in a frenzy. Galloping beside me Chris put the horn to his lips, and the spine-tingling staccato of his *gone away* struck my ears with a clarity and exuberance I had never, ever heard before in any single one of my Twenty Years in the Field!

We galloped on over the big, rolling Virginia fields as in a dream. The music of the hounds and horn, the wind, the rhythm of the horse under me comprised my entire world for those moments. Nothing else existed. Finally, in a field perforated by great clumps of holes, hounds checked. I watched as they cast themselves again, enthralled by the combination of breeding, instinct, and training that could produce a pack to work so skillfully and fluidly.

It wasn't long before they marked their fox to ground. In turn, hounds burrowed and scratched as far as their shoulders would allow in their effort to continue the chase. Chris slid from his horse and walked to the hole praising and petting his hounds. He put horn to lips once more, leaned over and blew the mournful, quavering *gone to ground* again and again.

The hour was late, and I knew we had seen the last run of the day. I had been up with hounds on this run from start to finish—practically part of the pack. The images and the hound music had seared themselves into my memory—memories I would always carry with me, even after the clock struck midnight and I would have to return to my "proper" place in the field.

4

IN THE TRACKS OF
MOUNTAIN AND MUSE

1998

I became acquainted with Dr. Roger Scullin, MFH, of the Howard County–Iron Bridge Hounds (MD) soon after I started publishing Covertside. *Roger was serving as a director of the Masters of Foxhounds Association at the time, and he invited me to be his guest for a day with hounds.*

I accepted with pleasure even before realizing how prominently Roger's hounds, his hunting country, and this particular fixture—Doughoregan Manor, a national historic landmark—figured in the early history of American fox-hunting. As a student of foxhunting, I dug into the subject and was immensely rewarded by what I learned. I hope you will agree that hunting in the tracks of Mountain and Muse would be a worthwhile part of anyone's foxhunting education.

Throughout the entire season I had looked forward to a day with the Howard County–Iron Bridge Hounds, thanks to the kind invitation of Dr. Roger Scullin, MFH. Here it was, late March and the last day of hunting. The temperature was in the eighties, it was sultry, and the sun was high. Fortunately for horses, hounds, and people there was a wind. Unfortunately for the huntsman, it was a south wind.

Nevertheless, it was a fascinating day following a pack that traces back to one of the defining chapters in American foxhound history and riding over countryside still in the hands of the family to which it was granted in colonial days. We rode in the footsteps of Mountain and Muse, the famous Irish hounds who were progenitors of the principal American foxhound strains—July, Birdsong, Trigg, Bywaters, and Walker.

We rode in the footsteps of Charles Carroll, a signer of the Declaration of Independence and said to be the richest man in the colonies at that time. And we rode in the footsteps of Charles Carroll's visitors, among them George Washington, Thomas Jefferson, and the Marquis de Lafayette.

Hounds met at Joint-Master J. Thomas Scrivener's farm near Clarksville, Maryland. The Scrivener farm adjoins Charles Carroll's former residence, Doughoregan Manor (pronounced "Doraygan"), now owned by Philip Carroll and still part of the original land grant of perhaps 20,000 acres granted to Charles Carroll by King George during colonial times. The entire day's hunting took place on the manor lands.

Charles Carroll is said to have extolled the glories of the chase one evening to several gentlemen, one of whom was General Lighthorse Harry Lee (father of Robert E. Lee), onetime governor of Virginia. General Lee "apparently agreed with everything that was said, but being in a rather negative mood, he innocently contributed the opinion that the sport could be most irritating 'if your nag is slow and your hounds are poor.' Quick as a flash Mr. Carroll turned on him and said, 'I refer, sir, to hunting in Maryland.'"[1]

MOUNTAIN AND MUSE

In 1814, the Duke of Leeds, who had married a daughter of Charles Carroll, gave two Irish foxhounds, Mountain and Muse, to a visiting guest from Maryland, Bolton Jackson. After Mr. Jackson returned to Maryland, he presented the Irish hounds to Colonel Sterrett Ridgely of Oakland Manor. Of Mountain and Muse, one admirer said:

> They were remarkable as are their descendants, according to the degree of the original blood, for great speed and perseverance, extreme ardour, and for *casting ahead* at a loss; and in this, and their shrill chopping unmusical

The imported Irish foxhounds, Mountain and Muse, as sketched by their savior, Benjamin Ogle, Jr. These images were reproduced from *The American Foxhound, 1747–1967,* by Alexander Mackay-Smith, having been published in that book through the courtesy of Col. Gwynne Tayloe of Mount Airy in Virginia. The original drawings became the property of the Tayloes through the marriage of Ogle's sister Anne to a member of the Tayloe family. The drawings are now the property of the Museum of Hounds and Hunting in Leesburg, Virginia, through the kindness of Mrs. Henry Gwynne Tayloe.

notes, they were distinguished from the old stock of that day; which when they came to a loss, would go *back*, and dwelling, take it along, inch by inch, until they got fairly off again, whilst these Irish hounds would cast widely, and by making their hit *ahead*, would keep their game at the top of his speed, and break him down in the first half hour.[2]

Although Mountain and Muse were prized for their ability to cope with the fleet, straight-running red fox that had been increasing in number since their importation and release in Maryland in 1730, Colonel Ridgely found them to be a handful to manage, and they came into the hands of Benjamin Ogle, Jr. (grandson of Samuel Ogle, Proprietary Governor of Maryland).

> Mr. Ogle told me [Mountain] was as famous for running dogs as foxes, and frequently he had so annoyed Mr. C.S.R. he (C.S.R.) at last directed his neck to be put *under the fence*—the common mode of executing a condemned dog. Mr. Ogle, seeing he was determined to kill him, asked not only for his life, but for the dog; and, in that way, preserved a most valuable breed.[3]

Benjamin Ogle, Jr., bred a pack of foxhounds from Mountain and Muse, including the famous Sophy whose portrait he hung in his library at Belair, the Ogle family's Maryland estate. From Belair, Mountain and Muse went to Charles Carroll, Jr.

> [Mountain] was a very compact dog, of middling size and what in cattle, in England, is called *flecked*, not spotted, with large dull blue grayish splotches—such at least was his appearance when I saw him at Homewood,[4] the residence of C. Carroll, Jr. to whom he had been presented by Mr. Ogle.[5]

The hound pair was finally separated when Mountain came into the possession of Dr. James Buchanan, who lived near Sharpsburg, Maryland. But Mountain and Muse had already produced foundation progenitors of the premier American hound types to come, the blood of which is still highly prized and carefully nurtured by today's preeminent foxhound breeders of both mounted packs and field trial foxhounds.

From Dr. Buchanan, Dr. Thomas J. Henry of Virginia (Patrick Henry's grandson) obtained Captain, said to be the greatest stallion hound of his day. When it came to speed and endurance, Captain had no equal, according to J. Blan van Urk. Highly inbred, Captain was by

Traveler out of Benjamin Ogle, Jr.'s Sophy. Both sire and dam were by Mountain out of Muse.[6]

When ordered south for his health, Dr. Henry took his pack from Virginia to Florida. Threatened by alligators in the bayous and lagoons,[7] they were taken back to Georgia. There Mr. G. L. F. Birdsong of Thomaston, Georgia, who had come into the doctor's life, became the proud owner of the, by then, famous *Henry pack*.

The results of this acquaintanceship and acquisition are the Birdsong or July hounds of Georgia (July having been the name of a hound tracing back to Captain[8] and belonging to Nimrod Gosnell, a Maryland farmer). The well-known Trigg hounds of Kentucky are also descended from the Henry Irish hounds.[9]

Nimrod Gosnell's farm, where July was bred, actually comprised a portion of the original "Manor Land" granted to Charles Carroll. George Linthicum lived nearby, as did John Hardy. Those three men founded the Howard County Hounds and created its first pack from their own Maryland (or Irish) foxhounds.

IN THE TRACKS OF HISTORY

Dr. Scullin, an ardent student of foxhound history and genetics, is one of the MFHA's chief resources in the area of hound care and breeding. The Howard County–Iron Bridge pack is a mix of American, Penn-Marydel, and Crossbred foxhounds. The American blood in the pack has been carefully preserved from what Dr. Scullin calls the Maryland or Eastern Shore hound, and what his predecessor, past-MFH Oliver Goldsmith, called the Irish hound. The Penn-Marydel was created by crossing that Maryland or Irish blood with the Pennsylvania and Delaware hounds. Because of the meticulous attention to the preservation of the old blood by Dr. Scullin and his predecessors, the great majority of the Howard County–Iron Bridge pack still traces directly back in unbroken strains to Mountain and Muse and to other Irish imports.

Before moving off, Dr. Scullin pointed to two young hounds,

littermates out of a Howard County–Iron Bridge bitch sired by a Green Spring Valley dog hound. The stamp of those prepotent Irish hounds, Mountain and Muse (high-set ears, snipey noses, white snips), after two centuries and countless generations, was still conspicuous in this breeding.

"Every so often we get a litter that looks like this, and they are wild to hunt!" said Scullin.

The hunting country about Doughoregan Manor is a mix of woods and fields. Virtually unfenced, hounds and riders move seamlessly from woods to fields in any direction without regard for obstacles. In addition to large wooded areas, there are numerous wooded coverts, separating the fields and narrow spits of excellent covert poking into or surrounded by fields, making for excellent viewing when a fox is found. Or a brace of foxes, as is often the case.

I was fortunate to be invited to ride up with Mrs. (Marion) Scullin, honorary whipper-in. Marion is the daughter of Albert Crosson, a former huntsman of MFHs Harry and Josephine Nicholas's Pickering Foxhounds in Pennsylvania. As hounds drew the first covert, Marion and I took a position at the edge of a small field in time to view our first fox cut across the corner. Hounds came together on the line but hardly had a chance to settle before the fox went to ground.

Our second view was in a large wooded covert at the edge of the property. The fox, whose attention was primarily on the hounds behind him, trotted in our direction until, spying us, he stopped, measured us for a moment, then ducked back into the woods to skirt us. If he hadn't turned, he would have been soon out of the hunting country. I suspect Marion knew his route pretty well. She had us in a perfect position all day and knew from long experience how the foxes run every bit of the country.

In fact, as we viewed our final fox away from a narrow spit of covert, Marion opined that, contrary to my belief, it wasn't the hunted fox. Once again she proved she knew her foxes and her coverts. We heard the horn from the other side, stood in the irons to ride, and the music that rose from this pack of traditional American and Crossbred hounds was a symphony to which we galloped at a steady pace over large rolling fields until the still soaring temperature took its toll on the possibility of further sport.

Surrounded by his pack and staff, huntsman Allen Forney called the roll, a unique final ritual to end the day. List in hand, one at a time, Forney called out the name of every hound that left the kennel that morning. The whippers-in scanned the pack after each name was called and sang out when they made a positive identification. I asked why they did this as opposed to simply counting.

"Many of our staff members are honorary, and this process is a terrific learning experience in identifying hounds," explained Scullin. "I saw Ben Hardaway do it at Midland, and I thought it was a great idea."

As Dr. Scullin, a Maryland MFH, acknowledged his debt to a pack in Midland, Georgia, so, almost seventy years ago, did George Garrett, foxhunter and author from Midland, Georgia, recognize the considerable influence of Marylanders on his beloved sport. In *Fifty Years With Fox and Hounds* (1932), Garrett wrote, "We must graciously concede to Maryland the glamorous distinction of being the royal nursery where the most eminent family of foxhounds in America was cradled and rocked."

NOTES

1. *The Story of American Foxhunting, Volume 1*, J. Blan van Urk, Derrydale Press, 1940, 1941, p. 39.

2. *American Turf Register*, February, 1832, p. 287.

3. Ibid., January, 1933, p. 234.

4. Homewood was the winter residence of Charles Carroll, Jr., now on the grounds of Johns Hopkins University.

5. *American Turf Register*, February, 1832, p. 288.

6. *The Story of American Foxhunting, Volume 1*, J. Blan van Urk, Derrydale

Press, 1940, 1941, p. 134, and *The American Foxhound*, Hayden C. Trigg, 1890, fold-out pedigree between pp. 80 and 81.

7. *Hounds and Hunting Through the Ages*, Joseph B. Thomas, MFH, 1928, p. 63.

8. Ibid., p. 64.

9. Ibid., p. 63.

5

HUNTING THE COYOTE *IS* DIFFERENT

1998

Jerry Miller, MFH, of the Iroquois Hunt in Lexington, Kentucky, and a past director of the MFHA was a strong believer in the association's new "reach out" experiment with Covertside. *As one who will put his time and treasure into that which he believes, Jerry did everything and more to help educate* Covertside's *editor. He invited me hunting often, and he took me more than once to experience the Peterborough Royal Foxhound Show. He also took me along for visits to some of the top kennels in England, where I saw hounds and bloodlines of the highest quality.*

Jerry didn't have to do any of that, and he probably wasn't doing it for me personally as much as he was doing it for foxhunting. Whether or not his generosity was well invested is for readers to decide!

Whipper-in [now huntsman] Lilla Mason turned in the saddle and said, "Be careful in this piece of country. You could get stuck in a bog."

"Lilla," I replied, "if I wind up in a bog, then you'll be in it too, because wherever you are, I'm going to be right beside you."

And I meant it. Here I was, a perennial member of the field, with the opportunity to ride up with the whipper-in across the Iroquois Hunt country near Lexington, Kentucky, for two consecutive days of hunting. *And* chasing the coyote! That was a first for me. I didn't plan to get left behind.

I had left home in the Shenandoah Valley of Virginia—where we are still fortunate to have an abundance of red fox—early the previous morning. It was not quite night, but not yet dawn when I slid behind the wheel, hunting kit in the front seat beside me, and drove out into the slush and snow. It was raining, the temperature was just below freezing, and the skies were leaden.

Iroquois huntsmen Jerry Miller, MFH, and Lilla Mason.   *Norman Fine photo*

With this inauspicious start, the doubts crept in. How many miles of freezing rain do I have ahead of me? How wet will it be tomorrow? How will the footing be? I slid a tape into the deck to put an end to it.

I had accepted a long-standing invitation from Iroquois Joint-Master Jerry Miller and his wife, Susan, and by the time I arrived at the Miller establishment later in the afternoon, the weather had cleared and the footing looked just fine. The door in the middle of the long veranda opened, and what appeared to be an entire pack of foxhounds came at me—some springy, some arthritic, some lame. Besides being home to favorite pensioners like Statesman 1992, the Miller house serves as a hospital for injured and recuperating hounds as well. And the Louisiana Catahoulas. They live there, too.

"Keep your bedroom door closed," warned Susan, "or you'll find hounds in your bed."

I closed it. The next morning, after breakfast, my host drove me around some of the Iroquois hunting country, then to the tiny town of Athens (pronounced with a long "A"). As we parked across the street from the only store in town, Cummins and Son, Miller explained one way he keeps in touch with farmers and landowners.

"If there's anything on their minds they want to talk about, they know they can find me here on Saturday mornings before the meet," he said.

Cummins and Son is a general store with a kitchen in the back and a few tables. Billy Cummins, the proprietor, was sitting behind the cash register near the front door. He interrupted his conversation with a couple of old boys at the counter to greet Miller as we entered.

Miller, a master of the exaggerated build–up, said to the assembly, "I want you to meet my friend Norman here. He's a famous writer."

Billy Cummins glanced at me.

"Did you wipe your feet?" he asked.

I guess some of us just can't carry it off. The old boys laughed with me, then launched into various subjects of local interest. Mrs. Cummins made Miller his usual chili dog sandwich, and we sat down at a table.

A large fellow came in, greeted everyone, then approached us. After a few minutes of conversation, in an offhand way, he got down to it. Apparently a group of farm workers had once again driven through a gate onto his field at night to party.

"Every time they do it, they leave me with a mess," he complained.

"We'll put a padlock on it. No problem," said Miller.

We said our goodbyes and left Cummins and Son. As we walked to the car, Miller explained that the Iroquois used his field for trailer parking at one of their fixtures, and although the farmer was kind enough to leave it open for them, it did create a nuisance for him. Miller pulled out his cell phone and dialed a number.

"We need to put a padlock on Craige's gate," he said to whoever answered. Then to me, "He would never have called me about the gate, but he knew I'd be here and he could chat."

At twelve-thirty in the afternoon, hounds, horses, and riders began gathering for the one o'clock meet. Miller introduced me to his Joint-Masters, Cathy Edwards and Dr. Jack van Nagell, the Iroquois staff, and many field members as well. Dr. van Nagell's wife, Betsy, a longtime Iroquois member, was graciously serving a stirrup cup of port, the official pre- and post-hunt beverage of the Iroquois, as it turned out.

My Saturday mount was a seventeen-hand, gray, three-quarter Thoroughbred cross named Furrier. Miller's horses are named after famous hounds. Lilla Mason buys and trains the Miller horses—mostly Thoroughbreds—and I had been told once by Miller that *all* his hunters go in a rubber snaffle. We may have been in a pub when he told me that. Not that I had any real reason to doubt his word, but after forty years of hunting I have found that facts relating to horses are more elastic than those pertaining to most other serious subjects. Sure enough, though, size and substance notwithstanding, Furrier was indeed equipped with nothing more than a rubber snaffle.

Miller, who usually hunts the hounds, was recovering from a nasty hunting injury, and hounds were being hunted by the young kennel huntsman, Phillip Stubbings, previously with the Exmoor in England. Stubbings has a sympathetic rapport with hounds and is a very quiet huntsman—more on the American style than the English.

Miller has bred a top-flight pack of foxhounds specifically to hunt the coyote—not just to chase it, but to *push* it. Midland MFH Ben Hardaway, in his book *Never Outfoxed*, wrote, "Jerry Miller and I are close friends, and he is a foxhunter—and one who is putting his money where his mouth is—sparing no amount of effort or expense in putting together one of the better packs of Crossbred foxhounds." Miller has used Midland Crossbred blood, which he mixes with some of the finest English bloodlines—not only from excellent English packs, but from the best lines in those packs—that particularly suit his aggressive style of hunting.

"Nose and drive are what I'm after," says Miller. "Speed follows. Hounds can only run as fast as their noses will allow."

Miller has paid his dues over the years—visiting England several times each season, hunting with the packs, attending the hound shows, getting to know Masters and huntsmen. He loves the Cottesmore blood especially for its drive and hunting intensity, and he has forged a close friendship with Cottesmore huntsman Neil Coleman. Miller also has Duke of Beaufort's hounds, including progeny of their famous Mostyn 1992. Other recent bloodlines in the Iroquois kennels are from the Cotswold Vale Farmers', Grafton, Berkeley, Bicester, North Cotswold, Exmoor, Vale of the White Horse, College Valley, and David Davies.

My host had said the night before that there was no such thing as a blank day when hunting coyote, and he was proved correct before long on this, my first day, at least. Hounds opened, and two coyote were viewed leaving the covert. Lilla was away at a gallop with me in her wake.

The first fence on a strange horse is always a question mark, but Furrier answered with a steady, confident, and workmanlike effort over the first coop. I sped after Lilla, who angled across the next field toward another distant coop at which we and Jack van Nagell, also riding as staff, were converging. With thirty years of conditioning as a field member, accustomed to giving way to staff and Masters, I began to throttle back as we approached the coop to allow van Nagell to precede me. He would have none of it, and with a grin, graciously waved me on ahead. I returned his grin, laid my leg on Furrier, and for the next two days never looked back. Both Furrier and my Sunday mount, Disney, galloped across the country, jumping flawlessly, never touching a fence, and responding to the slightest touch on their rubber snaffles.

Just as the red fox caused consternation among foxhunters during the nineteenth century as they slowly expanded their range, displacing the gray fox throughout the South, so now does the coyote, as he slowly displaces the red fox to satisfy his inexorable need for space. Just as our forebears were forced to make adjustments in their hounds and in their hunting methods, so now are we having to adjust again.

Mason Lampton, Joint-MFH of the Midland Fox Hounds (GA), speaking about hunting the coyote at a recent seminar of the Masters of Foxhounds Association, said that a complete change of attitude is required. The huntsman must expand his horizons, draw with the pack spread wider, send the whippers-in farther out, and plan on covering more distance at greater speed. He noted that the coyote differs from the fox in enough ways to require several changes of hunting strategy. One frustration arises from the fact that, unlike the individualistic fox, the coyote is a pack animal. When one is found, he is frequently in the company of others. As a result, hounds often split, and because of the speed and distances involved, there is precious little time to get them back together.

Lampton strongly recommended the use of radios when hunting coyote, primarily for the safety of the hounds. With the coyote running large five-mile loops, it becomes necessary to radio ahead if the pack is approaching a major road. He also recommended the use of road whips—individuals in vehicles, in touch by radio, who can drive quickly to an anticipated road crossing to stop hounds. This coyote hunting strategy includes the necessity of naming all the coverts and areas of the hunting country so that those broadcasting the location and direction of the pack can be specific and succinct.

This day's events were to ratify all that Lampton said. Both coyote must have run together for a short way before splitting. The pack split as well. The radio that had been slipped into a holder on my saddle began to crackle.

"They're running west toward the interstate," reported Joint-MFH van Nagell.

"We'll drive ahead and stop them at Cleveland Road," replied the voice of ex-huntsman Pat Murphy in the hound truck.

With the prospect of hounds being stopped by the road staff to prevent them from crossing a major highway, Lilla swerved from the action and galloped back in search of the hounds that had split. I followed. As if radios weren't enough of an innovation, she suddenly plucked a cell phone from her pocket and, holding reins, hunt whip, and radio in one hand at the gallop, calmly dialed a number. Apparently Miller's radio wasn't working, so she gave him a status report by calling his car phone.

Lilla is a splendid whipper-in, continuously scanning the pack, swinging to and fro, making corrections before problems develop. For a perennial field member like me, the mileage logged by a hardworking whip in the course of a hunting day is astounding. We finally came upon the errant hounds, and Lilla set about collecting them. She called, wheedled, and coaxed with great patience and eventually rendezvoused with huntsman Stubbings and the main pack. In due course, another coyote was found, and we had a good chase to end the afternoon.

Visiting the kennels afterward, I was particularly struck by the depth of quality among the dog hounds. I expect bitches to be generally more attractive than dog hounds, but in the Iroquois kennels, both sides of the aisle showed extraordinary class.

Miller likes a big hound. That gives him a big frame upon which to hang a lot of muscle, needed to sustain the drive, speed, and stamina for pushing the coyote. Marty Wood, MFH of the Live Oak Hounds (Florida), often warns breeders to pay close attention to size. Wood claims that it's easy to breed down in size, and much more difficult to maintain or breed up.

The Iroquois hounds hunt on Wednesdays, Saturdays, and Sundays. Wednesday and Saturday meets are formal, and horses are braided. The Sunday meet is ratcatcher, usually a shorter day, and more of the young entry are used. This is one hunt where the working folk get a break; they can hunt twice a week. On nonhunting days during the season, hounds are kept to a rigorous fitness schedule, going out morning and afternoon, routinely logging a minimum of eight to ten miles a day.

The country is mostly open—large grazing pastures for cattle and tobacco fields planted in a winter crop such as wheat, which gets plowed under in the spring. It is gently rolling like much of the Virginia hunting country. Creek bottoms are firm, so crossings are reasonable mostly everywhere. And, thanks to the coyote, there are very few groundhog holes—perhaps the *only* benefit to sportsmen bestowed by this great predator.

The next day, Sunday, the meet was scheduled for two p.m. at Jack and Betsy van Nagell's Brookfield Farm with a bitch pack consisting mostly of puppies. I was mounted on a big bay Thoroughbred named Speed and Drive, also equipped with the standard-issue rubber snaffle. His stable name was Disney, however, which tended to calm any trepidations suggested by his more intimidating formal name.

I joined up with Lilla again, and we set out at a trot on the right flank, perhaps seventy-five yards behind the huntsman, hounds spread before him. Stubbings suddenly kicked his horse into a gallop and cheered hounds forward. There, in the middle of the field ahead, disdaining the nearby covert, was a coyote—the first find of the day—spotted by the observant huntsman. The pack converged on the line with tremendous cry, and we enjoyed our first chase over a lovely piece of open country.

Disney was buttery smooth into and over his fences and would shorten or lengthen his stride to the obstacles at the asking. Clearly, his education exceeded what is generally required in the hunting field, and I later discovered that he was a local celebrity at horse shows and combined training events in the off-season. He was a joy to ride, as was Furrier the day before, and I was able to watch hounds undistracted.

Stubbings drew the coverts at a trot. Lilla and I were usually out on a flank, and I was able to watch hounds at their work. It was quite different from the often painstaking and careful search for the elusive fox. Hounds trotted briskly through the coverts with the attitude that if a coyote was there, he'd get up and go, and they'd know it. In each case, the find was not signaled by a tentative whimper of a hardworking hound as so often happens with the fox, but rather an eruption of cry from many voices simultaneously, followed immediately by an explosive pursuit.

After a final run of perhaps thirty minutes over the rolling Iroquois countryside behind their lively and active young pack, Masters and staff called it a day. For me, two days back-to-back of hunting up front with hounds was a treat to be savored, along with the last and sweetest glass of port.

6

OPENING MEET AT BELLE MEADE IS BOTH JOYOUS AND SERIOUS BUSINESS

1999

The first time I hunted at Belle Meade I was hooked. The addiction came easily. Master and huntsman Epp Wilson is charismatic—the keenest foxhunter and gamest sportsman you will find, with an exuberant personality, a flair for drama, and the knack of becoming a lifelong friend after a day in his company.

His Joint-Masters, Charlie Lewis and Gary Wilkes, hunt staff, hunt members, and all their families are devoted to the hunt and to the way of life that the hunt provides. Since most all of the meets start and finish at the kennels, the hunt clubhouse—Boots Hall—is a home away from home for the entire establishment. Epp could undoubtedly be elected mayor of Thomson, Georgia, in a landslide if he chose to run.

We met when Epp was serving as a director of the MFHA. He suggested that his Opening Meet might be different from anything I had experienced in Virginia, and he invited me to see for myself.

In Thomson, Georgia, they know when Belle Meade holds its Opening Meet. You just can't hide one thousand people in Thomson. Nor do hundreds of out-of-towners filling motel rooms and restaurant tables go unnoticed. It all started thirty-four years ago, the hunt's very first year, when James E. Wilson, Jr., MFH, decided to invite neighbors, landowners, and friends to join in the Blessing of Hounds and to follow the hunt in tally-ho wagons. Belle Meade has staged this special day every year since for two worthy reasons: to make friends for foxhunting by sharing and demonstrating the joy of their sport *and* to raise money for the hunt. Lots of money.

There *are* foxhunting purists who deplore the notion of staging a foxhunting demonstration for a throng of partygoers, but the concept works in Thomson because for the rest of the hunting year, the Belle Meade subscribers hunt the fox and the coyote behind one of the finest packs of Crossbred foxhounds in the country *and* in accordance with the highest traditions of the sport. It also works year after year because the Joint-Masters—James E. Wilson, his son, Epp Wilson, and Charlie Lewis—are held in the highest esteem by their hunting members and by their community. Indeed, many who have moved from Thomson to other parts of the country come back, year after year, to man their old jobs and help make a success of this special day in Belle Meade's hunting year.

The big moneymakers are the tally-ho wagons and the book. This year, a record 728 people, most of whom paid thirty dollars each for the ride, piled into more than thirty wagons, many decorated, pulled by all manner of tractors and pickup trucks. These wagonloads account for over twelve thousand dollars of net income to the hunt.

The book, a picture-filled yearbook of the previous year's activities, is unveiled on Opening Day. Of the two thousand that are printed, many are distributed at the weekend events, but many are also used by the local Chamber of Commerce, by local businesses, and by the local hospital in its recruitment packages for doctors. The book contains stories of special hunts, profiles of honored individuals, trips taken by the Belle Meade hounds to other hunting countries, reprints of articles about the hunt, and reminders concerning hunting etiquette and correct attire. Member lists, hound lists, and landowner lists are included. And the advertisements—well over a hundred—net another ten thousand dollars.

The proceeds from the tally-ho wagons feed the foxhounds for the year. Advertising revenues from the book have, from day one,

Epp Wilson, MFH and huntsman, with the foxhounds of the Belle Meade Hunt.
Debbie Turner photo

been reserved for capital needs such as kennel repairs, hound truck and trailer, and the like.

IMPRESARIO WILSON

I arrived the afternoon before the big day and was met at the airport by Lucy Bell, a foxhunting attorney who, when she moved to Thomson, inserted a clause into her employment contract ensuring that she may hunt on Wednesdays. We pulled up to the farm just as a riding and jumping demonstration by four young ladies for the benefit of the Spruce Creek Flying Club had ended. (Did I mention that twenty-one private planes of the Spruce Creek Flying Club landed at the McDuffy County Airport that day filled with guests for the Belle Meade festivities?)

As laid-back and relaxed as Epp Wilson appears to be, there is something of the Barnum & Bailey in him. While Epp was showing me around the farm, the young ladies who had just finished giving the riding and jumping demonstration were cooling their horses in a field of permanent schooling jumps. At some invisible signal, two of the four girls peeled off, cantered toward us, jumped a big log fence abreast, and halted in front of us.

"I'd like you to meet Mandy and Kim," said Epp nonchalantly.

As we completed our hellos, the two remaining girls hooked up at the canter, jumped the same fence abreast, and halted before us.

"This is Susannah and my daughter, Wendi," said Epp.

In the very next moment, a boy on a pinto pony, energetically waving one arm over his head and using his voice like a hunting horn, came galloping into view followed by six hound puppies. The small huntsman and his miniature pack disappeared from view only to reappear in a few minutes still in full cry—the boy, not the puppies.

"That's my son, Chase," Epp explained. "He takes care of the hound puppies, exercises them every day, and teaches them to follow."

Epp's wife, Sharon, met me with a hug—my first conventional greeting of the day.

THE DAY UNFOLDS

Guest status is wonderful. You succumb to the wind and currents and allow yourself to be carried along—no chores, no responsibilities. The day begins with an enormous buffet breakfast at the Belle Meade Country Club (no relation to the hunt): eggs, biscuits, bacon, sausage, and cheese grits.

Over breakfast I chat with an attractive out-of-town couple full of questions about foxhunting. How did this Harvard-educated attorney and his wife happen to be there? I ask.

"We bid on it at a silent auction in Atlanta, and won!" says the wife.

I would see them at various intervals during the day, and their curiosity, enthusiasm, and sense of adventure never flagged. Chalk up new friends for foxhunting.

Time to mount up. I am privileged to be asked to ride to the Blessing of Hounds with huntsman, hounds and staff. As we approach the site of the blessing, I get my first view of the enormous crowd assembled there. The logistics had been planned and executed well ahead of time by Epp's tireless volunteers, and everyone—wagons, spectators, honored guests, mounted field, and presiding pastor—are in place and ready for us. Master, hounds, staff, and your reporter make a grand entrance by jumping a coop into the field, then walking into a perfect V-formation of dismounted riders and horses—more than forty on each side of us—toward the waiting pastor.

Rev. Edward R. "Father" Frank has been performing the blessing ceremony every year since the beginning, thirty-four years ago. He hunted with Belle Meade and senior Master James Wilson for many years, and although he has given up riding, his enthusiasm and love for the hunt still glows. Father Frank begins by relating to the assemblage the story of Saint Hubert and how he became the patron saint of hunters. He then invokes the blessing, copies of which have been handed out so that all may participate in the responses. We then, each and every one of the mounted riders, come forward to receive our own Saint Hubert medal from Father Frank. Many will carry the new medal with them through the entire season, then add it to their collection of medals from prior years—each a unique design to commemorate the occasion.

Time to remount. We move off with hounds, staff, and field. The first exhibition of the day is a drag hunt for the benefit of the crowd in the tally-ho wagons. And it takes a considerable amount of time, no matter how well organized, to move 728 people and park them so they can see. The radio finally crackles that all is ready, and we jump into a field where the drag has been laid. Hounds do their part, running and speaking to the line in full view of the assembled wagons. Cameras click, videos whir, and huntsman, staff, and field follow the hounds around a pond in this natural amphitheater. We complete the segment by jumping the final panel toward waiting photographers and gallop to a finish between the two rows of parked wagons.

While the wagon train moves to the next location and assembles to view the final drag, Master Epp takes the opportunity to hunt for live quarry. At Belle Meade, chances are fifty–fifty of finding either fox or coyote. Although he never served in the Navy, Epp has adapted a system of station-keeping for his staff's formation. At all times, he wants hounds and huntsman in the middle and whippers-in at each corner, ahead and behind. To help "keep station," each wears a wrist compass.

After drawing for a short while through a thickly wooded covert, hounds open with a glorious sound—much different from their notes on the drag!—and we are treated to a nice burst of action. A whipper-in reports viewing a coyote, but with the noise, traffic, and confusion of the day, neither the coyote nor the hounds seem to be able to settle down to their respective duties.

The final segment brings hounds, staff, and field to their conclusion at the top of a hill in the midst of the hunting country, where, miraculously, a graciously laid table of hors d'oeuvres and champagne materializes. Hot and perspiring after hours in the broiling sun under wool hunt coats, we gratefully accept the sparkling beverages proffered.

"Welcome to Champagne Hill," says Epp.

7

HUNTING ON THE BORDER

2000

Although I had hunted in England, my education was incomplete according to my friends Matthew Mackay-Smith and Cliff and Laura Hunt. I had never hunted with the English and Scottish Fell packs. To remedy that void in my experience, they convinced me to join them on their annual pilgrimage to the Border Country. There I discovered another mode of hunting altogether, and I shall be forever grateful to them, for it was not to be missed.

As an ordinary member of the field, how does *your* dream hunt unfold? In mine, there's no Field Master. I jog right up to the huntsman's side where I can be in close touch with the pack. And if I get ahead of him when hounds are running, he smiles and says, "Go on!" It happens there *is* such a place, and you don't have to fall asleep (or die) to get there.

This most unorthodox hunting takes place in the vast, wild, and unspoiled Cheviot Hills in the Border region of England and Scotland, the gritty inhabitants of which stopped even the Roman Empire in its tracks northward. Early in the second century A.D., the Roman Emperor Hadrian built his famous wall of stone from coast to coast, seventy miles long, fifteen feet high and six feet wide, running just south of these hills, to protect his citizens from the northern "Barbarians."

Later, in the fourteenth century and for a period of almost four hundred lawless years thereafter, the Border region was a scene of thievery, midnight raids, rustling, and murder to a degree that renders

A typical view for the Border country: Forty or fifty miles of grass, heather, gorse-covered hills, and planted forestries all the way to the undulating horizon.

the American Wild West tame by comparison. Over the very hills where today's foxhounds run, on dark nights, the Border Reivers, both Scottish and English, rode out on their speedy Hobbies, tough little sprinters bred for racing. Cannily picking their way around the treacherous peat bogs on the tops, clad in leather jerkins and steel helmets and armed with lance and sword, they descended swiftly out of the blackness upon the sleeping inhabitants of a farm, or often upon an unprotected widow, gathered up all they could carry, drove off the sheep and cattle, set fire to what remained, and sped away, hiding their stolen herds in natural bowls between the hills.

Today, the descendants of these ancient families and clans are a sturdy, wiry lot, spare with words and quiet of voice. They hunt a demanding country to which they have been bred for thousands of years. To the newcomer it offers a continuing series of challenges. Though there is little jumping, there are long hills that leave horses gasping and rattling for air, with deep bogs on top and steep descents. Parts of the country offer broad, clean, springy turf for galloping, but there are other parts where no two strides are alike.

Also bred for this demanding country are the Fell hounds. I caught my first glimpse of this old and unspoiled breed as they made their appearance with Michael Hedley, MFH and huntsman of the Border Hunt. My first impression was that I could be looking at a pack of American hounds. They seemed slighter of build than their sturdy English cousins with somewhat slender, but not snipey, noses. I found further evidence of the American look in Daphne Moore's book *Foxhounds*, where she wrote, ". . . the Fell hound stamp of head, which, in its purest form, has the high occipital bone, resulting in a pronounced dome."

The Fell hound is independent, wide-ranging, and has a strong voice. Nothing less would answer. The scale of open space on the border country is so vast that hounds must draw widely and often hunt on their own with little help from the huntsman. Great cry is required because hounds may be out of sight behind a hill, and the frequent winds shred lesser sounds inaudible. And this is one hunting country where hound color is important, white hounds being of great value when the huntsman is squinting out over many miles to locate his pack.

I was with a party of American friends: Matthew Mackay-Smith, veterinarian, editor, publisher, and lifelong foxhunter; Ernest Benner, veterinarian and first-time foxhunter; Herb Jonkers and Tom Walker, both businessmen and experienced foxhunters; and Cliff and Laura Hunt, a couple who have devoted their lives to hunting and for years have organized annual trips to the English border where they take up temporary residence in a cottage in the Border Hunt country. Our horses were provided by Johnny and Hilda Wright of the Redesdale Arms hotel in Rochester. They were well schooled, sure-footed, fit, and up to the task. And the tack was good.

The hunting was like no other I have experienced: a combination of unique country—open, hilly, varied, vast; a country that lays out the action—the foxes and the hounds—in full view; an unorthodox style of following, combining the best of hilltopping as well as racing after hounds—rider's option; smaller fields and a more relaxed attitude than what would be encountered with the more formal English hunts; and finally, extraordinary foxhounds with all the speed, drive, and hunting intensity anyone could hope for. It is a place for those who ride to hunt because hunting the fox is the purpose, and much of what happens transpires in full view. Those who hunt to ride may find their dream hunt elsewhere. Not that we didn't have our fine gallops, but much of the country is rough—lumps, bumps, ups, downs, ditches, mud, and bog—oftentimes all within a few strides.

The biggest lesson I learned my first day out was how to save my horse. Matthew doesn't care if his horse stands or fidgets, walks or jigs, so long as when hounds are running the horse has the stamina and heart to keep up over that fatiguing terrain. I soon learned why he was content to put up with his horses' antics. Hounds had found, and, although we could hear them, we couldn't see them because fog had settled in. Nevertheless, Matthew was off and running. Ahead of him was Peter, a local fellow who whips-in to Master Hedley. I had been warned of the peat bogs, but I figured it would be safe to follow since Peter was leading the way. I gave the mare her head and we galloped after the music, down one long slope and up the next. The fog was getting thicker, however, and my mare was falling behind.

The next hill undid her entirely, and I began learning how to economize on pace to let her wind return. My pilots, however, had disappeared on ahead. Alone in this unfamiliar, limitless terrain with little visibility, I resolved not to be so quick to follow Matthew again. Fortunately, the Fell hounds made themselves heard quite adequately, and I was able to keep up by ear. Trotting and sometimes walking up the hills then cantering down, occasionally getting a reassuring glimpse of a horse and rider ahead disappearing into the fog over the next crest, I stayed in the race and finally caught up to Matthew and Peter in a dell between two hills at the edge of a forestry into which fox and hounds had disappeared. Giving this fox best, it was a full thirty minutes before we three saw another soul—time to nibble on a few bits of cheese I had stuffed into my pocket—and another thirty minutes for Master Hedley to collect hounds for the next draw.

Contiguous to the Border Hunt country and hunting over similar terrain on both the English and Scottish sides are the West Percy, College Valley & North Northumberland, Duke of Buccleuch's, and the Jedforest—all excellent packs showing wonderful sport. Highly prized throughout the hunting world, College Valley bloodlines are to be found in many of the best packs on both sides of the Atlantic.

On my final day with the Border, a joint meet with the Ullswater was scheduled. The Ullswater is a foot pack that hunts the Cumbrian Fells in the Lake District. It was a pleasure to see John Harrison again, ex-huntsman of the Toronto and North York Hunt (ON), who had returned home from Canada to become huntsman of the Ullswater. There were perhaps twenty mounted followers for this joint meet, another twenty on bikes and ATVs, and 141 automobiles (somebody counted!) looking like a thin column of ants on the roads below.

As hounds plunged down the slope before us to draw a heathery covert bordering a narrow stream, we meandered up the long open slope above them where, when we gained the top, we had the typical view for this country—forty or fifty miles of more grass, heather and gorse-covered hills and dales all the way to the undulating horizon. No houses or buildings, just scattered flocks of sheep—little white slow-moving dots in the distance—and, in the valleys, ancient stone circular sheep stells with a single opening into which the sheep can escape the occasionally ferocious winds that scour the hillsides.

A fox slipped out of the heather ahead of hounds, scampered along the stream for a way, then made for open country—he had little choice—striking out up the next hill and traversing its length in full view before us. Hounds trailed up to where he had been lying and opened with a roar. We had the option of saving our horses and watching from the hilltop as Master-and-huntsman Hedley was doing, or leaving him behind and careening on down after the hounds. Either way is okay with him. He has radio contact with his mounted whippers-in and with his terrier-men riding mountain bikes and ATVs. He was in no hurry. It was just after eleven a.m., and he wouldn't be thinking of quitting until about five p.m.

I chose to be patient this time and save my horse, and was rewarded with a fifteen-minute chase that took place in full view of our hillside. The fox maintained a good lead initially, but as the two packs started working as one, they began to press him. Hounds were checking less frequently, and the fox decided to double back. He hurried down the opposite hill toward us and disappeared into the heather fringing the brook. Only momentarily, though, because hounds owned his line and, all together, were gathering speed down the hill toward his sanctuary.

The fox broke out, making for the slope below us, and tore up our hill just barely ahead of the clamor. Hounds had him in sight and had switched to high gear. The lead hounds were no more than fifteen feet behind and closing the gap by a couple of feet with each stride. With only one more stride before being rolled over, the fox darted to his left and, as hounds hurtled past his turn, disappeared into the hole he alone knew was there.

Before the day was done, Michael Hedley and John Harrison would kill five foxes, to the great satisfaction of the sheep farming constituency there.

"I told you this pack was a fox-killing machine," said Matthew, not so subtly reminding me that he and the Hunts had been urging me for several years to accompany them on their annual visits to this part of the hunting world.

So how does a dream hunt end? With food, of course. Where else will you find a horse purveyor furnishing a tailgate tea? As Johnny took the horses from us at the end of each day, Hilda was there with a picnic basket of sandwiches, fried chicken, tea, coffee, homemade shortbread, and cake. Just enough to hold us until we got back to the cottage, changed, and went out in search of lamb shanks and Scotch whisky.

8

NEW LIFE AND AN OLD HAND FOR THE ROLLING ROCK HUNT

1999

I have served as editor of The Derrydale Press Foxhunters' Library for more than ten years now. In that capacity and to my great pleasure I finally came to meet a world-class huntsman behind whom I had ridden in Ireland early in his career. Hugh Robards, huntsman of the County Limerick foxhounds for twenty-seven seasons, had emigrated to the United States to become Joint-MFH and huntsman of the Rolling Rock Hunt in Ligonier, Pennsylvania. Robards, publisher Jed Lyons, and I were working at the time on Hugh's won-derful first book, Foxhunting in England, Ireland, and North America, *which Derrydale published the following year.*

(At the time of this writing, Robards is huntsman of the Saxonburg Hunt in Pennsylvania.)

Institutions, like people, have their ups and downs. The Rolling Rock Hunt in Ligonier, Pennsylvania, was down, and the Masters were determined to restore it to its former position of prominence on the American sporting scene. At the same time, on the other side of the Atlantic, Hugh Robards was down, having just been sacked after twenty-seven years as huntsman for the County Limerick in Ireland. How the Rolling Rock and Robards came together at their nadirs and charted a common course toward a fresh zenith is an in-spiring story.

Their mutual revival started just two years previously, in 1997. The once magnificent Rolling Rock Hunt kennels, situated on the grounds of the Rolling Rock Club and built in the grandest manner of the 1920s, were deteriorating. With the Hunt unable to maintain the kennels to acceptable standards, the Club was about to take them over and use the structure for another purpose.

The Joint-Masters—Mrs. Burt K. Todd (who was retiring), Thomas Slater, and H. Phipps Hoffstot—invited Mrs. Armour (Sophie) Mellon to serve with them as Joint-MFH. It had been banker/industrialist Richard Beatty Mellon of Pittsburgh, a brother of Andrew Mellon—financier, industrialist, and Franklin Roosevelt's Secretary of the Treasury—who had built the Rolling Rock Club in the early years of the twentieth century as a gunner's and angler's paradise. It was R. B.'s son, Richard King Mellon, who started the Rolling Rock Hunt and brought it to the pinnacle of American sport in the 1920s and 1930s. With young Mrs. Mellon aboard, the four Joint-Masters shared a dream of reviving the once proud tradition of the Rolling Rock Hunt.

In New York for her first Masters of Foxhounds Association Dinner, Mrs. Mellon stood alone, not knowing a soul. Al Schreck, ex-MFH of the Los Altos Hounds in California and ex-MFH of the County Limerick foxhounds in Ireland, spied this attractive lady and introduced himself.

As their conversation drifted to mutual misadventures while trying to hire huntsmen, they were astonished to discover that they had each made an offer to, and received an acceptance from, the same huntsman! They decided on the spot to dismiss that option, and it was then that Schreck had a matchmaking inspiration. He told Mrs. Mellon about an English-born huntsman in Ireland, unemployed at that moment after a lengthy career hunting the well-known County Limerick foxhounds.

The Rolling Rock Joint-Masters invited Hugh Robards to Ligonier for an interview. Then they addressed the remaining pieces of their puzzle. They proposed to the Hunt Committee that the Mellon family would make up the hunt deficits; kennels would be rebuilt; Hugh Robards would be engaged as Joint-MFH and huntsman; the Hunt Com-

Hugh Robards, MFH and huntsman, with the foxhounds of the Rolling Rock Hunt.
David Pollock photo

mittee would be dissolved; subscribers would no longer vote; and the
Rolling Rock Hunt, once again, would be a private pack. The proposal
was accepted by the Hunt Committee.

For Robards, the move and transition had to be bittersweet.
English-born though he is, he loves Ireland and considers it his
home. He had spent his career breeding hounds for, and hunting
them over, an open, soft, lush, and moist country. Ligonier is in
western Pennsylvania in the Allegheny Mountains—part of the Ap-
palachian range that runs southwest from Maine in the northernmost
latitude of the United States practically to the Gulf of Mexico. Now
he would be starting from scratch in a foreign land of hills, woodlands,
and hard, gravelly footing. Yet he had to be buoyed by the prospect
of hunting hounds again.

"I had just arrived and was familiarizing myself with the hounds
that were left in kennels," Robards said. "Sophie kept asking when I
would take the hounds out. Finally, one day I opened the kennel
doors. Hounds went flying in every direction. It was clear I had to
start over."

He recognized early on that although he adored the old English lines going back to the Belvoir and the Brocklesby that he bred and hunted at the County Limerick, he needed hounds with two special characteristics: great cry so as to be heard when they couldn't be seen and conformation that would stand up to the hard footing and the steep hills.

Robards is quick to express his gratitude to MFHA Executive Director Dennis Foster, who worked with Mrs. Mellon and her Joint-Masters to help bring him here, and to several American Masters who sent him good hounds. Live Oak (FL) MFH Marty Wood got on the telephone and asked Masters around the country to draft good hounds to Robards. He has received hounds from Live Oak, Green Spring Valley, Millbrook, Elkridge-Harford, New Market–Middleton Valley, and Blue Ridge. He has also received hounds from Sir Watkin Williams-Wynn's in England and from the Duhallow, Louth, and Tipperary in Ireland.

Although he referred to his new hounds as the United Nations pack because of their disparate bloodlines and type, he is now feeling confident about the sort of foxhound he wants and is breeding some of the old English bloodlines back into the pack. For one thing, these are lines that he knows intimately, and for another, it is Mrs. Mellon's dream to bring back the sort of hound that R. K. Mellon obtained from the leading English kennels of the 1920s with the help of his friend, George Evans, MFH of the Hampshire.

Although Robards and I had never met, I have had his photograph hanging on my wall at home for thirty years in what turned out to be a case of mistaken identity. In 1971, my wife and I were on our then annual hunting trip to Ireland. One day with the County Limerick, just before mounting up, I spied who I thought was Lord Daresbury, then MFH, sharing a joke with his new young huntsman, Hugh Robards.

"Quick, Joanie," I said urgently to my wife holding the camera. "Get that picture of Daresbury."

Later, back home, when the films were developed, I chose that wonderful portrait of the MFH to enlarge, frame, and hang on the boot room wall with our other memorabilia.

Now, thirty years later, as editor of The Derrydale Press Fox-hunters' Library, I was to meet Hugh and work with him on the publication of his brilliant memoir. Just before one such meeting, I showed Robards my old photograph of him and who I had long supposed was the inimitable Lord Daresbury.

"Oh, yes," he said. "That's me and Lord Harrington." I took the picture home and hung it up again, but it's different somehow. Not that Lord Harrington wasn't most probably a perfect brick. And it's not as if I even *knew* Lord Daresbury. It's just . . . well . . . after thirty years on my wall, I thought I *did* know him.

A GOOD HUNTSMAN NEVER LOOKS BACK

Last season I revisited the Rolling Rock, along with seven of my fellow Blue Ridge Hunt compatriots from Virginia, and found such progress and harmony as to warm the heart of any romantic soul. Blue Ridge Joint-MFH Linda Armbrust and Terry Chandler were re-visiting country they had known as children. Don and Prue Anderson, Lynn Cathcart, Vail Juhring, and Eric Myer rounded out the Blue Ridge contingent.

The Rolling Rock Masters had scheduled back-to-back meets Saturday and Sunday for us visitors. We arrived on Friday afternoon and settled our horses into hunt stables on the Club grounds. The stables are managed by Krissy Weaver who, on hunting mornings, after supervising the tacking up of some half dozen horses, speeds to the kennels, dresses, and mounts her own hunter to help whip-in to Robards. After a strenuous day in the field, it's back to the barn where she's not through until tack is cleaned and the hunters are groomed and fed. As will unfold, this was to be no small task for her late Saturday afternoon when I returned with my horse.

Friday evening, the Robardses—Hugh, wife Caroline, and daughter Emily—hosted a sit-down dinner for fifteen at their long, lustrous dining room table set with silver and crystal, all brought across the Atlantic with them. On Saturday morning an elegant stirrup cup served on silver trays by white-jacketed waiters in black ties was waiting for us in front of the venerable Rolling Rock Club. And even though Derrydale publisher Jed Lyons was unable to be there that weekend to hunt, his empty house was commandeered by his sister-in-law, Katy Jones, for a hunt tea on Saturday afternoon. We were thoroughly spoiled by the hospitality of our Pennsylvania neighbors.

My personal plan was to hunt on Saturday and take photographs on Sunday. I had brought my old campaigner, St. Nicholas, a sixteen-hand bay Thoroughbred, and Robards invited me to ride up with him and the hounds on this bright and crisp Saturday morning.

I love watching a professional at the top of his game working, whether it be a bartender, heavy equipment operator, or huntsman. There is a rhythm, a flow, a grace, an intuitive touch that operates on a plane higher than that of the spectator. Hounds had been drawing the woodland covert for a while, when suddenly Robards pointed with his horn to one hound. Moments later that hound was the first to speak.

"Good girl, Silver," he said with warmth. "Try on, my hearts."

Hounds continued on through the bottom land toward a creek. Sterns started feathering, and several more hounds began speaking tentatively.

"That's a curious line, isn't it?" muttered Robards, watching his hounds closely then gazing beyond, left-handed. To me, it was all random motion. Yet I suddenly had a flash of insight that, while I only saw where the fox *had been* by watching hounds, Robards saw where the fox *was going*. It seemed that he could project the fox's perambulations ahead of hounds like some dotted line on a map.

We continued at a walk, crossing the creek, as hounds continued working toward the base of a steep ridge. Huge fallen trees, the hardwood trunks polished to a gleaming finish by the weather of countless seasons, lay askew in our path. Hounds worked steadily up the ridge, then left-handed around the hill, picking up their pace. We galloped around to the other side on a good gravel path, stopped, and heard hounds working toward us from above. Hounds crossed the gravel, silent and feathering, and continued down the hill. Commander, a handsome Crossbred dog hound from the Live Oak, spoke on the other side. The others honored and agreed. They had it now.

"G'dog, g'dog," Robards cheered. He blew some quick notes on the horn to let the field know we were on the move.

Robards had explained that when hounds run in this country you had to cut corners or risk losing them entirely. We pelted down the hill through stands of whippy trees, often bushwacking from one path to pick up another. We galloped on, the pack in full cry ahead. I followed Robards through several stream crossings, all firm gravelly footing underneath. We came to another stream by an abandoned shack. Robards went around to the left of the shack and crossed. I waited to allow a few hounds to cross, saw very little room for Nick and me to squeeze between the trees, the thick vines, and the shack, and decided there was more room and a good shallow crossing on the right. Big mistake!

Nick stepped off the bank and immediately sank into a bog to his chest. There was no bottom. He followed with his hind feet and was good and truly stuck. I jumped off, pulled the reins over his head, and scrambled back onto the bank to get my weight off his back. The poor horse thrashed and floundered and finally stopped, exhausted, lying half submerged on his flank in the muck. Robards and the hounds had disappeared ahead.

I hadn't a clue where I was, or how, or even if, my poor Nick would get himself out. He's such a proud-looking horse, my heart ached to see him so helpless and uncertain. I let him rest a bit, then encouraged him to try again. The boggy area was evidently small. He was able to get his forelegs free and stretched out in front of him, on firm footing but still underwater, before he lay back exhausted again. I let him rest, then we tried again. Finally, with a series of tremendous heaves, he got his hind end out. He was plastered with mud to the saddle, and I didn't know if he had pulled any muscles, so, for both of those reasons, I refrained from remounting and started off on foot to lead both of us out.

Anyone who has ever hunted with me will attest that I'm always lost, even in my own hunting country. I led Nick in the direction I thought the field might be. I took a fix on the sun and determined to keep it over my right shoulder, but the trees and growth were so thick, we couldn't make progress in a straight course. It seemed that every direction I headed I wound up getting Nick tangled up in the thick vines.

Some fifteen minutes later, I totally surprised myself by actually finding the field. They had been thrown out of the race by the terrain and had lost touch with the pack—as happens occasionally in that difficult country. Considering the state Nick and I were in, we were a surprise to the field as well. What a strange sight we must have made when the field and I finally arrived back at the kennels: Mrs. Mellon and I riding tandem on her horse, Ivy, with Nick, riderless and plastered with mud, ponied behind.

Robards and hounds didn't arrive back at the kennels for another forty-five minutes. I told him my wife would never forgive him for abandoning me in a bog, but he was too flushed with the success of his hounds to care. They had finally put their fox to ground.

The Rolling Rock Hunt kennels and grounds are once again a source of pride. The Masters are striving to live up to the traditions of their early history. The new MFH and huntsman, Hugh Robards, who trained under some of the greatest huntsmen of the last half century (Brian Gupwell, Captain R. E. "Ronnie" Wallace, and Charlie Wilkin, to name a few), bred a world-class pack of foxhounds for a quarter of a century, and hunted them over as physically demanding a country as will be found anywhere, is surely up to the task. Richard King Mellon should be proud.

9

PETERBOROUGH 2001

The Year of the Rain and the American

This was also the year of England's tragic epidemic of foot-and-mouth disease. Seven million sheep and cattle were destroyed—perhaps 80 percent of which were healthy animals—in an attempt, eventually successful, to curb the epidemic. Besides the unimaginable pain of killing their own healthy herds, bloodlines nurtured and refined by generations of farming families were lost forever.

To prevent the spread of infection, the countryside was basically closed down. All hunting was curtailed, and traffic between farms was discouraged with strict disinfection procedures in place. The British countryside was distraught.

Aficionados of English foxhunting and hound breeding will not soon forget their 113th Peterborough Royal Foxhound Show, held on Wednesday, July 18, 2001. Separate deluges, both morning and afternoon, distracted hounds and created a muddy lake in the holding area where handlers and hounds stood waiting to enter the ring. And a 122-year-old tradition* was ended when C. Martin Wood III, MFH of the Live Oak Hounds of Monticello, Florida, entered the ring just before ten o'clock in the morning to judge the dog hounds. In so

---

*Shows were not held during the two world wars.

doing, Wood became the first American ever to be invited to judge that most prestigious of all hound shows. His co-judge was David J. Palmer, MFH of the Worcestershire (UK).

Although Wood, in his pin-stripe suit and bowler hat, was indistinguishable from the rest of the officials, there was a restlessness in the air that bespoke something new and different. Even possibly unpleasant! One lady to whom I relinquished my seat for a short time early in the day said, her voice ringing with reservations over the entire prospect, "I suppose he'll pick hounds that look American." I tried to reassure her that Mr. Wood had, in fact, seen English hounds many times before. The fact is, of course, that Wood had already judged all the other major hound shows in England and North America, but up until this watershed (pun intended) year, Peterborough remained as it had always been—exclusively British.

Captain Ronnie Wallace, MFH of the Exmoor, perhaps the best-known genius of English foxhound breeding, was one of several of his countrymen who strongly encouraged Wood's ordainment among his peers. The fact that not all were convinced was less a matter of confidence in Wood's judging skills but stemmed more from long-held tradition.

To be fair, most of the people I spoke to were enthusiastic about the American judge. *Horse and Hound* editor Arnold Garvey said, "It's good. We need outside people coming in. I'd have them every year. We should have had Hardaway here years ago."

Michael Hedley, MFH of the Border (UK), was also supportive, despite throwing a low blow. "I think it's a good thing," he said. "Marty is an experienced judge. And if he gets it wrong, his wife will tell him so."

Indeed, Daphne Wood, the other Live Oak Master, having judged three of the five major English shows herself, and frequent judge at North American shows, was seated in the front row in the midst of all the luminaries of British hunting: Sir Luke Annaly, Captain Charles Barclay, James Barclay, Lady Jane Beritsen, Frank Houghton Brown,

C. Martin Wood III, MFH of the Live Oak Hounds in Monticello, Florida (right), was the first American invited to judge the prestigious Peterborough Royal Foxhound Show. Wood and his co-judge, David J. Palmer, MFH of the Worcestershire (left), judged the dog hound classes in the morning.   *Jim Meads photo*

Ms. Felicita Busby, Hugo Busby, Sam Butler, Simon Clark, Adrian Dangar, Captain Brian Fanshawe, Captain and Mrs. Ian Farquhar, Michael Hedley, Lady Caroline Gosling, Mrs. R. D. Green, Mrs. P. T. Humphrey, Mr. and Mrs. Alistair Jackson, Major Sir Rupert Buchanan Jardine, Mr. and Mrs. Martin Letts (the former judged the bitches in the afternoon), Ian McKie, Sir Philip Naylor-Leyland, Mr. and Mrs. Nigel Peel, Martin Scott, Peter Stoddard, Richard Summer, Tim Unwin, Mrs. Elizabeth Verity, Edmund Vestey, and Captain Wallace.

Wood, who had never attended the Peterborough show before, admitted it was an awesome experience when he first entered the ring and became conscious that among the spectators were, as he put it, "the panoply of everyone who was anybody" in the British hunting firmament.

The Peterborough Royal Foxhound Show is held under a roofed pavilion at the East of England Showground in Peterborough, about one hundred miles north of London. The images absorbed by a first-time visitor are very much the same as would have been seen 123 years ago on the occasion of the first Peterborough show. Dark suits and black bowlers are de rigueur for the male members of the Peter-borough Royal Foxhound Society, while extravagant hats adorn many of the ladies.

This year's show was the biggest in years if not ever. Twenty-seven packs entered 755 hounds, of which about 360 were exhibited before an appreciative audience of perhaps five hundred—mostly Masters, ex-Masters, and Association officials. Colonel John Parkes, MBH and hound trustee for the Ashford Valley, commented that it was the best lot of hounds he'd seen in twenty years. Visitors from the United States included Jerry Miller, MFH, and Lilla Mason, huntsman of the Iroquois Hunt (KY).

Later, relaxing at ringside after his baptism while Martin Letts, MFH, and A. C. Cook, MFH, judged the bitches, Wood reflected on what for him had just constituted the high-water mark of his judging career. "The standard here is so high," he said, still in wonder like a kid in a candy store. "The first thing I'll do when I get home is go to the kennel, pull all my hounds out, and look at each one in the light of the standards I've seen here."

"There may be fewer total hounds here than the 750 hounds ex-hibited at the Virginia Foxhound Show," Wood said, "but there are four rings going there. This was all in one ring. We had fifty-four hounds to judge in one class. In the two-couple class the ring was so crowded there wasn't room to move."

I remarked to Wood of the great number of extravagantly beautiful movers in all the classes.

"I breed for movement and I judge for it," Wood replied. "That should always be the deciding factor in a championship. The hounds placed themselves. What we're looking for is an athlete. Once the key pace and stamina points are evaluated, I then move on to the quality of activity and balance. Finally, I look at the movement of a foxhound which is his great fluid beauty. A hound that does not move well cannot do his job for very long."

The hound show at Peterborough acquired its exalted status from King George V in 1934, when permission was granted for the title of the sponsoring Society to be the Peterborough Royal Foxhound Show Society. The show has often been attended by members of the royal family. Last year, the Society mailed Queen Elizabeth the Queen Mother special congratulations and loyal greetings on the occasion of her one-hundredth birthday, which she graciously acknowledged, expressing how she has enjoyed her visits to the Peterborough Show over the years.

Hounds are shown by hunt staff dressed in formal hunting attire. Boots are boned and polished, and hounds were pristine at the start, but after a couple of hours of downpour white britches were splotched with muddy paw prints and streaked with scarlet dye running from new hunt coats.

Staff wear armbands on their right sleeves indicating their hunt affiliations, and the winning handlers tie their large prize rosettes onto their left sleeves and wear them proudly throughout the day. The arms of multiclass winners become festooned with color.

The affair takes place under a roofed pavilion that shelters both exhibitors and spectators. The show ring is bordered by a white, wooden enclosure about three feet high. Several rows of seats in three levels surround the enclosure. At one end is an elevated platform supporting the scoreboard, which is manually updated throughout the day with the names of the winning hunts.

Peterborough winners provide a standard against which all breeding efforts can be compared. The Society asserts that its judges "concentrate on the conformation of hounds, selecting those which they

FOOT-AND-MOUTH DISEASE

Reminders of Britain's tragic battle with foot-and-mouth disease were ever present at Peterborough. The first reminder hit as you entered the show grounds. Thick mats perhaps three feet by six feet in size were positioned at the narrow show entrances so that everyone entering or leaving had to walk on them. The mats had a porous top surface. Inside was a spongy foam material saturated with a disinfecting solution. Walking on them forced the bubbly mixture up around the soles of the shoes. Many ladies wearing sandals had their bare toes and feet disinfected as well! The foxhounds betrayed yet another reminder of the foot-and-mouth epidemic. "The condition of the hounds showed the effects of the closing down of the countryside," observed Wood. "They didn't have that finely chiseled musculature."

No wonder. When hunting was voluntarily terminated last February by the British MFHA upon confirmation of the outbreak of FMD, hunts were no longer allowed to collect fallen stock from the farms in their hunting countries. With little flesh available, many of the hunts have switched to feeding kibble. Wood, who feeds a combination of kibble and ground chicken necks to his own pack, believes there is a transition period that the hounds must go through as their systems adjust to the absorption of protein in a different form, before they start rebuilding muscle.

Another reason for lack of fitness has been the inability to exercise hounds over the roads and the countryside as they did before FMD. Many hunts are just exercising hounds in their grass yards. Even those hunts that are able to exercise freely are reluctant to do so for public relations reasons in the local farming community. No one knows when hunting will be allowed to resume this season, and hunt staffs are reluctant to get hounds too fit too early.

feel are best able to work effectively in the hunting field. A hound's colour is irrelevant, and there is no attempt to judge for fads and fashions." It is the highest honor to be asked to judge at Peterborough. When a pack wins a rosette there it becomes a permanent landmark in that hunt's history.

10

HUNTING WITH MELVIN IN THE ALLEGHENIES

2001

During Covertside*'s early years, I spent many hours at the National Sporting Library in Middleburg, Virginia, researching material for articles. At that time, the Sporting Library was located in the old* Chronicle of the Horse *building (the old Vine Hill mansion, now under renovation and scheduled to house the new National Sporting Art Museum in 2011).*

To reach the Library, you entered the Chronicle *building and descended a stairway to a low-ceilinged basement—sometimes damp, sometimes hot, depending on the season. From that basement room, in order to reach the stacks, you descended yet another step or two directly into the office of director Peter Winants and librarian Laura Rose.*

There was always a smile of welcome from these two, and before pursuing my mission, whatever it was at the time, I would spend a few moments chatting. In the fall, Peter would often regale me with the exploits of the recently formed Bath County Hounds and their incomparable huntsman Melvin Poe. I was entranced. And then, one day, I was invited!

When the invitation came for two days of hunting with the Bath County Hounds I leaped at the chance. Not because the Bath County Hounds are so famous. They're not. They're a small, private pack. And not because their country is better than my home country for fox-hunting. It's not. It's hilly and wooded, while mine is open and gently rolling. Why then? Because it gave me the chance to hunt once again behind the legendary Melvin Poe. In foxhunting circles he is referred to simply as Melvin. Like Michael in the NBA.*

Melvin grew up in the Virginia countryside. He was the boy to whom his friends turned to identify trees, birds, and animal tracks. His father, uncles, and friends were all enthusiastic hound breeders and hunters.

Melvin retired in 1991 after more than forty years as a professional huntsman, the last twenty-seven years as huntsman for the famed Orange County Hunt in Virginia. His pack of red ring-necked American hounds was one of the premier packs, and a day in their superb hunting country south of Middleburg was highly sought after by visiting sportsmen and women from both sides of the Atlantic. Yes, I remember the great runs when visiting the Orange County, but what stands out most in my mind is how Melvin's hounds adored him.

We've all seen huntsmen hustle their hounds back onto the hound truck after a hunt, the theory being: capture them while they're still here. Not so Melvin. After hunts at the Orange County, he just allowed hounds to hang out. They weren't about to leave; they were where they wanted to be—with him. The door to the hound truck always remained open while Melvin offered his homemade wine to the foxhunters. Some hounds would climb in; others would lie on the ramp or at his feet outside. They were relaxed and happy, and, if they weren't snoozing, their eyes followed his every move in complete adoration. That wasn't training. No one, not even Melvin, can *train* hounds to do that. That connection is made from somewhere deep inside.

After his retirement, however, Melvin was pretty unhappy. Even his wife, Peggy, declares he's more like a foxhound than any other creature. What was a brilliant hound man like that to do? The former longtime

---

* Around the turn of the century, there was a professional basketball player—arguably the best to ever play the game—named Michael Jordan. With a winning smile, personal character, and charisma to match his unsurpassed skills, he was so admired that he was universally referred to by sports announcers, fans, teammates, and even opposing players simply as Michael.

Melvin Poe takes the Bath County hounds across the Jackson River to the first draw. *Joan Fine photo*

chairman of the Orange County Hunt, George L. Ohrstrom, Jr., had the answer.

FOXHUNTING RETURNS TO BATH COUNTY

Mr. Ohrstrom owned a farm, Fassifern, deep in the Allegheny Mountains of Virginia, which he had purchased in the early 1980s as a sort of "getaway" place. Fassifern is located in the town of Warm Springs in stunningly beautiful Bath County, so named for the hot sulphur springs that over two centuries ago made the area a desirable destination for wealthy vacationers seeking the cure. The famed resort hotel, The Homestead, originally established in the late 1700s, still welcomes guests to this quiet and naturally magnificent locale tucked away far from civilization.

In the late 1800s the then-owner of Fassifern kept a pack of foxhounds there, which he organized as the Fassifern Hunt Club. Later, in 1934, the Masters of Foxhounds Association of America recognized the Bath County Hunt, organized by Rachel Ingalls, owner of The Homestead. Mrs. Ingalls hunted the drag pack and W. Burling Cocks, later to become a Hall of Fame steeplechase trainer, alternated as huntsman of the live pack. The Bath County Hunt expired with the advent of World War II, but after the war The Homestead began to host annually what became a highly popular A-rated horse show and competitive trail rides, the latter enduring to this day.

With a sporting and hunting heritage already well established in Bath County, it occurred to Mr. Ohrstrom that he was in a position to bring foxhunting back to Fassifern and to provide a new purpose for Melvin. He established his private pack, the Bath County Hounds, in 1992.

His plan was welcomed by most of his neighbors, such as the Hirsh family, who own neighboring Meadow Lane, a 1,200-acre farm and popular lodge for anglers and nature lovers. Still visible on the Hirsh farm are the remains of historic Fort Dinwiddie. Built to protect English settlers from Indian attacks and to provide an outpost against the French, the fort was visited by George Washington in 1755 while serving in His Majesty's Colonial Forces.

However, one neighboring landowner was unhappy with Mr. Ohrstrom's plan to revive foxhunting, especially over her land. Mr. Ohrstrom had the answer for that problem, too. He bought her farm, all six hundred acres of it. In fact, Mr. Ohrstrom is so charmed by Fassifern and Bath County, that he has, over the years, accumulated other farms and properties to the extent that now, from the farmhouse where his hunting guests stay, the long view up the valley—across the trout-stocked Jackson River, over patches of dark woods and lighter green fields, for three miles to the distant greensward rising to the final crest—is all his. Having assembled this precious expanse of natural wilderness and open space, Mr. Ohrstrom is currently in the process of placing the entire holding into conservation easement for the enjoyment and appreciation of sportsmen and women in perpetuity.

THE BATH COUNTY HOUNDS

The Bath County Hounds meet every two weeks from early September to mid-November. Wednesday is a travel day to Fassifern. Hounds meet Thursday morning and again on Friday morning. After a final hunt breakfast at the farmhouse, everyone returns home on Friday afternoon.

With apologies, this reporter found it difficult to pin down the cast of characters at the Bath County Hounds. No one admits to any official capacity except for Melvin, who, at age eighty-two, is the undisputed huntsman. Peter Winants, past editor of *The Chronicle of the Horse* and past executive director of the National Sporting Library, when pressed, acknowledges that some individuals refer to him as the MFH. John Coles, a Joint-MFH of the Orange County Hunt and Fassifern's major-domo for the hunting guests every fortnight, whips-in to Melvin.

Hunting in Bath County has been uniquely challenging, according to Winants, whose book, *Foxhunting with Melvin Poe*, debuts this fall. The first couple of years there were very few foxes, but Melvin instituted a fox feeding program that solved that problem. The hills, ridges, and steep gorges make it difficult to hear hounds, and when they are heard, the sound often comes from directions other than where hounds are. And the shaley soil is not ideal for holding scent. Nevertheless, Melvin and his hounds provide wonderful sport in the old-time southern tradition.

The Bath County experience begins on Wednesday. While some guests choose to trailer their horses directly from their home farm to Bath County, others, under John Coles's direction, load their horses onto Mr. Ohrstrom's Whitewood Farm van at The Plains, Virginia, for the three-and-one-half-hour drive. A passenger car or two, loaded with luggage and people, complete the convoy. Melvin and Peggy drive hounds, Melvin's horse, and two days' supply of vittles.

After horses are unloaded and tended to, the remainder of Wednesday evening is reserved for cocktails—perhaps some of Melvin's wine—and a grand farmhouse dinner prepared by Peggy. If weather and time permit, guests may, drinks in hand, play a few games of croquet before dinner. Melvin's rules are employed. What are they? You never know in advance; they are decreed as needed during the progress of the game.

Sharing the farmhouse this week, besides the regulars—Poes, Winants, and Coles—were Ginevra (Ginny) Hunter, ex-MFH of the Los Altos Hunt in California; Tommy Lee Jones, huntsman for the last thirty-two years of the Casanova Hunt in Virginia and a popular sporting writer; and my wife, Joan. Mr. and Mrs. Ohrstrom are usually present as well, but this week only Mrs. Ohrstrom, Jacqueline, was able to come. She arrived in time to brighten the dinner hour, hunted on Thursday, then returned home Thursday afternoon to prepare for a driving show on the weekend.

OCCASIONALLY THE TRUTH IS TOLD

After dinner, over a nightcap or a glass of Melvin's wine, tall tales are told. Like the time Melvin's hounds trailed up to a black bear, the weight of which, first estimated at three hundred pounds, had grown to five hundred pounds at the hunt breakfast, and had turned into the biggest bear Melvin had ever seen by dinner time. Occasionally the truth is told as well. Like the time Tommy Lee Jones at the age of twelve blew a hole in his foot with a .410-gauge shotgun, *through* which he could watch his programs on the television at the foot of his bed while convalescing.

Hounds met at eight on this cool and rainy Thursday morning. John Coles, recovering from a foot injury (no shotgun involved), was not able to whip-in, but Tommy Lee proved to be a more than adequate substitute, even though it was his first time in that country.

Typical of many American huntsmen, Melvin uses the horn sparingly—primarily to call hounds to him. The rest of the hunting day he uses his voice in a variety of screeches that range from the caw of an angry crow to the sharp bark of a fox. His hounds understand him perfectly.

Melvin and nine-and-a-half couple of hounds forded the Jackson River for the first draw—a cornfield near the stables—which was immediately productive. Longtime Shenandoah Valley foxhunter Joe Conner viewed a big dog fox out of the cornfield headed for the woods and a steep-rising cliff. Hounds opened with a roar and the field galloped up the first of many hills via a series of switchbacks. We were able to stay in touch with hounds after emerging into the open at the top by jumping a snake fence, then following the cry back down to the big open bottom land where hounds finally lost after about twenty-five minutes.

In this country, many of the valleys and plateaus are cleared and open for farming and livestock grazing, but the steeper hills remain wooded. Paneling has been added over the years to improve access. Excellent rides are maintained throughout the wooded tracts, and Smasher—my big-striding, 16.3-hand Thoroughbred—leveled out and came back to me pretty softly after a couple of those long hills. The woods are mature with a good canopy that keeps the undergrowth down, so visibility is good through the woods. Some trails are carved into the sides of steep wooded slopes, where the trail's edge may drop dizzyingly for more than a hundred feet into water-filled gorges below. There are places on the trails where the rider looks *down* into the treetops and hopes his horse is sure-footed.

After breakfast and a short rest, Melvin went grape-picking for next year's wine. Though he looked for volunteers to help, the rest of us, junior in years but no match for his energy, had other plans. We went off to the baths.

THE JEFFERSON POOLS

Thomas Jefferson, who in 1818 sojourned in Bath County for over three weeks and soaked in the Gentlemen's Pool House three times a day, pronounced the waters as being "of the first merit." Coles, Jones, Winants, and Fine—bobbing about inside the same ancient wood clapboard structure in which Jefferson soaked (built in 1761)—agreed. The spring waters are crystal clear, mineral-rich, and naturally warm. Gaseous bubbles rise from the rocks ten feet below, producing a faintly pungent sulphurous atmosphere. The two ladies, Hunter and Fine, enjoyed their hour in the separate Women's Pool House.

The weather was greatly improved for Friday's meet. The day was misty to start, diffusing the early light through which softly rounded hills rose smoothly from the wet meadows. Melvin drew the same cornfield, but the fox had been on his feet earlier. Hounds found his line in the woods and trailed him toward the cliff once again, but lost.

Back on top, hounds found again and were running strongly, but down toward a dangerous hardtop road over which trucks, heavily loaded with fresh-cut timber, often roll. Melvin said later that Tommy Lee asked if he should go down to the road and stop hounds.

"Before I could answer, Tommy Lee had already disappeared," said Melvin.

Tommy pelted down the gravel drive and reached the road just ahead of the hounds and was able, fortunately, to stop them.

On top again, in the woods at Upper Fassifern, hounds opened below us. Staff and field waited to see what direction the race would take, but, though hounds were clamoring, they didn't seem to be going anywhere. Melvin worked his way down on foot and found the denned fox staring at him from beneath a large rock.

It was that kind of a day. Hounds found their next fox in the briars on the Haynes farm. (Bebe Haynes is a lean and fit foxhunting mother of five, to whom I am forever in debt for outfitting me on a previous visit after I had left all my tack—saddle, girth, bridle, and breastplate—back home.) Melvin, thinking this was a gray fox, was about to whip hounds off to save them from getting torn up in the briars, when Tommy Lee viewed it away. It was a red, and it gave us a nice run before giving hounds the slip.

We finished up in the bottom land near the river with the sort of hunt I particularly love. Say what you will about the thrill of a long, fast gallop, and I'll agree. But I also love the chance to stroll or trot along with hounds on a difficult scenting day and watch them find, lose, cast themselves, try, find, and lose again—boo-hooing slowly along—in the slowly warming flush of an early autumn morning. For an ordinary member of the field like me, it provides a rare chance to really see hounds work.

Everyone, besotted with the ambience and natural beauty of Bath County, lingered over Peggy's final breakfast, loath to leave. Reluctantly, after hugs, words of thanks, and promises to come back, the convoy began its return trip out from the Alleghenies, back across the Shenandoah Valley, and on to the Blue Ridge and home.

11

A FLY ON THE WALL

Inside the Ashford Valley Hunt for the Liberty and Livelihood March

2002

One hundred foxhunters from North America journeyed to London to support their English foxhunting cousins in a mass protest of the British government's threat to ban foxhunting. Thirty-five chartered trains and twenty-five hundred buses brought more than four hundred thousand country people to London for the largest civil rights protest in the history of the British Empire.

I wanted to see and report the event from the English viewpoint, so rather than join up with the American contingent I stayed with English friends and tried to be a fly on the wall.

Friday, September 20, 2002. Bethersden (near Ashford, Kent)

4:00 p.m. I arrive at Potter's Farm in Kent, home of my hosts, Ian and Lynne Anderson, MFHs of the Ashford Valley. As I pull into the farmyard, I see Ian on a ladder mounting floodlights. I learn he has just been burgled. Is it connected to the fact that he was included in a "hit list" published by the Urban Alliance, a militant antihunting group? He tells me the police don't think so.

Ian and Lynne discovered the burglary upon returning home from Spain and the World Equestrian Games early afternoon of the previous day. The police were called at 1:30 p.m., and they responded at

9:30 p.m. Slow response and a lack of protection by police officials all over the country turn out to be a frequent topic of conversation among many people I speak to in the hours and days to come.

I will learn that England has embraced the philosophy of political correctness to the extent that police officers are reluctant to inject themselves into any situation requiring physical contact. Although England does have laws against harassment, police do little to enforce them. When hunt saboteurs disrupt hunt meets, pull children off ponies, bloody horses, direct aerosol sprays at hounds' noses, the antis videotape everything, waiting for a response from the foxhunters or the police. If there *is* a physical response, it is caught on tape, the provocations are edited out, and the tape is furnished to the broadcast media. A police officer "guilty" of performing his duty finds himself brought before a committee of inquiry defending his job and his future.

Ian remains intent upon finishing the installation of the floodlights, because we are due at Leeds Castle for the Wye College Beagles Autumn Ball that evening, and the farm will be unattended.

Leeds Castle, Maidstone, Kent

8:00 p.m. We arrive at the ball after great care is taken in locking and securing Potter's Farm. The ball takes place in the Terrace Room directly across the moat from Leeds Castle. Listed in the *Domesday Book*, the castle has been a Norman stronghold, a royal residence for six of England's medieval queens, a palace of King Henry VIII, and, in the eighteenth century, the home of the Fairfax family. It was Thomas Sixth Lord Fairfax who left this magnificent castle in the 1740s to come to the Shenandoah Valley of Virginia and assume control of his inheritance, five million acres, the entire Northern Neck of Virginia. Fairfax sent foxhounds in advance of his arrival, hired sixteen-year-old George Washington to help survey his holdings, and, together with young George, enjoyed foxhunting in the very country now hunted by the Blue Ridge Hunt. Since Blue Ridge is my home hunt and Fairfax's Colonial home site is not five miles from my farm, I feel a remote connection to the castle.

To experience the Liberty and Livelihood March from the English perspective, I joined Ashford Valley Hunt Joint-Masters, Ian and Lynne Anderson (right), on a special train chartered by the protest organizers to bring them and their hunt supporters from Kent into London. The Andersons, whose names appeared on an animal rights "hit list" that threatened property damage to their farm on the day of the march, blocked the driveway to their farm with their horse box. Daughter Tory (left), somewhat apprehensive, stayed behind at the farm to stand watch. *Norman Fine photo*

During the course of the evening, I hear stories of hunt sabotage that boggles my American mind. One Master of Beagles tells me of a man who prowls his front yard at two a.m., a ski mask concealing his face. I would love to have been able to suggest to the prowler that he try that stunt in West Virginia, but didn't have the chance. I am told another story of a police officer standing idly by while a hunt saboteur wrestles his fellow officer, a woman, to the ground. His reason for inaction? "I have a wife and child at home to think of," he was heard to say.

Upon returning to Potter's Farm, Ian advises that I lock my car and lock myself into the guest house.

Saturday, September 21, 2002

6:30 a.m. The Ashford Valley hounds are meeting for a day's hunting, and I am privileged to be mounted on Lynne's favorite horse, Moon, an ex-trotter with a very fast, *big* trot. The fixture is at a farm of two thousand acres—wide open with many small coverts. It is autumn hunting, and the huntsman wants coverts held up. Hounds find quickly, and the fox breaks by the whipper-in. Hounds are running the line and I'm riding point with Ian. Moon is steady and kind. We follow hounds and find ourselves at a small holding—house and garden—where the fox has evidently passed. Hounds are working to regain the scent, and as Ian and I approach we hear the screaming of a young teenage girl.

"Get out of my garden! Get out! Get out!" she yells. Her mother joins her as we draw near.

"Your hounds have killed a fox in my garden," she accuses Ian shrilly.

"No, madam. The hounds haven't killed a fox," Ian replies calmly.

"They have. There's blood on that one's leg," she insists.

"The hound has scratched himself in the briars, madam. It's his own blood," Ian says.

"Are you saying you don't kill foxes?" she persists.

"Yes, madam, we do kill foxes. The farmer that owns this land wants foxes culled. But we haven't killed a fox today," Ian says.

"You're just a bunch of bloody . . . (she struggles to choose an appropriate word for us) . . . people . . . with nothing better to do with your time," she yells.

So here we are—the crux of it. The words she almost blurted out were "rich toffs." It irritated me. I didn't feel rich. I was wearing twenty-five-year-old field boots, the soles and heels of which have been replaced more times than I can remember. My hacking jacket was given to me by a friend twenty years ago.

I want to ask her if she likes to go the movies when she has spare time. I want to tell her that I don't go to movies. I go foxhunting. But what's the use? We resume hunting. As we leave, we hear her blistering the hapless whipper-in as he unsuspectingly comes up behind us.

It is hot and dry—unusual for England—and scenting is difficult. As hounds finish drawing a large covert blank, Ian and I come across a couple on foot, man and woman.

"What are you up to?" the woman asks.

"Oh-oh, here we go again," I think.

"We're foxhunting, madam," replies Ian.

"Well, I can see that!" she says. "Is this regular autumn hunting? Yes? That's fine. We're marching tomorrow."

Whew! Lose one, win one.

4:00 p.m. The Ashford Valley foxhounds meet again, this time on foot, at Boughton Place in Grafty Green. Autumn hunting here is a time not only for training young hounds but for culling foxes as well. A field of about twenty foot followers accompanies staff and hounds as the first covert is drawn by a quiet road. Hounds find quickly and the fox is viewed by foot followers holding up the covert. Scenting seems better at this time of the day, and huntsman Neil Staines crosses the road and descends a long hill toward the next draw. The view from the road is spectacular; the entire country to be hunted is spread out below us in full view; grass fields and small coverts unfold for more miles than I hope to walk.

I fall into conversation with a field member, Betty Chantler, and learn she is the Countryside Alliance's Train Coordinator for the southeast of England. She has arranged the booking and taken passenger reservations for the three specially chartered trains, each pulling nine carriages, that will transport nearly three thousand marchers to London tomorrow from the southeast. Other marchers around the country will travel to London on chartered and scheduled trains and coaches as well as private automobiles. The chartered coaches alone, if placed nose to tail, would cover fifteen miles of roadway.

Hounds perform well and kill one fox for the landowner.

Sunday, September 22, 2002. Day of the Liberty and Livelihood March

9:00 a.m. We eat a hearty breakfast because we don't know when we will be able to eat again. The Andersons' daughter Tory (short for Victoria) will drive us to Pluckley Station where we will board the chartered train for London.

Tory is nervous this morning. Considering the recent burglary and the fact that the Andersons were named on the Urban Alliance's hit list of people who, it was threatened, might suffer damage to their property on the day of the march, her anxiety is understandable.

"Nothing will happen, Tory," Ian assures her. "The police are aware of the situation, and will come out if you need them. If anyone does come here, just go upstairs and call 999."

Before leaving for the station, Ian removes the sign identifying the farm and parks the horse box in the driveway near the road to block any vehicles from entering.

11:00 a.m. Hunt members, staff, and other local farming families are gathering at Pluckley Station to await their chartered train. It is a good-humored crowd that includes children and elderly men and women.

11:15 a.m. The train arrives on schedule. Ian and Lynne secure an excellent first-class compartment that we share with a local couple and their two sons. A train official comes through and explains a change of plans necessitated by the huge crowds collecting on the London streets. Instead of disembarking at London Bridge as planned, we will go one stop beyond to Cannon Street Station. Ian pulls out his cell phone and begins calling others on the train, including his Joint-MFHs, to coordinate the new arrangements.

1:00 p.m. We arrive at Cannon Street Station, unfurl the hunt's banner, and emerge onto the street. It is chockablock with people and sound. Banners are held aloft identifying hunts and organizations. Signs—some humorous, some angry—express prohunting sentiments, farmers' complaints, and generally negative opinions of the Blair government. Hunting horns blare and people cheer. Whistles pierce the air. The weather is beautiful—sunny and warm—and the immense crowd, though in excellent humor, is determined to be heard.

Countryside Alliance stewards are at all the train and coach stations to direct the marchers. Our group falls in with the crowd and begins a slow shuffle toward the starting point. Approaching a construction site, we follow the uplifted gaze of the marchers ahead and see about six construction workers high above us on the steel skeleton of a rising structure overlooking the street. The workers are putting on a skit for our benefit. One holds a large sign upon which is boldly printed, BAN HUNTING. After the crowd has a good chance to express their feelings with boos and catcalls, his fellow workers attack him in a mock battle and wrestle him to the floor. Pumping their arms in the air in victory, they accept the cheers of the crowd. As the final act, the "anti" gets up, turns his back to the crowd, and moons us. More good-humored cheers and shouts. After moving down the road a bit farther, we hear the crowd behind us first booing, then applauding, and know another performance is taking place before a new audience.

3:30 p.m. We have shuffled slowly in a circuitous route for two and a half hours, covering very little distance in total, finally reaching our official starting point at Blackfriars Bridge on the Victoria Embankment by the Thames River. Banners and signs are hoisted with renewed vigor. Hunting horns and whistles, cheers and shouts erupt in earnest as we make our way along the embankment; down Whitehall Place past policemen and women who applaud us; past the mounted Horse Guards, whose horses stoically tolerate even this incredible crowd and din; past Downing Street from which Prime Minister Blair is absent; past the Cenotaph, where, at the behest of the Countryside Alliance stewards, the boisterous crowd falls respectfully silent as they pass this sacred memorial to Britain's "Glorious Dead"; thence to the finish at Westminster under the long-seeing gaze of Big Ben. What history that corner has witnessed—wars, victories, controversies, and celebrations. And what notables Big Ben has gazed upon through the ages—world leaders, great and evil, exalted heroes and treacherous fools. And we are part of that history—England's largest civil rights demonstration ever.

4:15 p.m. As we pass through the official finish point, counters above us on scaffolding tally the marchers with handheld electronic counters as we funnel through. Immediately before us an electronic tote board, displaying the tally in real time, reads 343,141 as we finish. Before the march is over, the count will reach over four hundred thousand. The marchers are all ages, from children to the elderly. They are on foot, aided by canes, and pushed in wheelchairs.

We decide that the easiest way to return to the train station will be to cross Westminster Bridge and circle back from the opposite side of the Thames. Halfway across, Ian points out a crowd of Americans. In the middle of the bridge, waving their flags and wearing sweatshirts emblazoned "Americans for Foxhunting," is a contingent of the many Americans who had come to support their British friends, among them MFHA President Daphne Wood, MFH, Live Oak Hounds (FL), wearing a stars and stripes baseball cap; husband Marty Wood, MFH and past-president of the MFHA, hunting horn in hand; Penny Denegre, MFH, Middleburg Hunt (VA), holding a sign proclaiming "Life, Liberty and the Pursuit of Happiness"; and Christian Hettinger, designer and producer of the international foxhunting symbol.

5:15 p.m. Back in the Cannon Street Station I buy an ice cream and a bottle of water, the first scrap of nourishment I've had since breakfast. In less than thirty minutes we are on the train heading back to Kent.

8:00 p.m. Back in the kitchen at Potter's Farm, drinks in hand, we tune in to the news for coverage of the events of this incredible day.

The BBC calls it "a phenomenal success." Alun Michael, Minister of Rural Affairs, is interviewed next. He tells the viewing audience, "I'm not sure what [the marchers] are trying to say. . . . The decision [regarding hunting] will be based on the evidence and principles. Today's activities should not influence us."

With due respect, Mr. Michael, there is no question what the marchers "are trying to say." The Countryside Alliance has long since made public the credo of this Liberty and Livelihood March in which they demanded that government (1) defend the rights of rural people to live their lives responsibly in the way they choose, (2) safeguard rural people from prejudiced attacks on hunting with dogs and all other field sports, (3) respect the values and customs of rural communities, (4) ensure any laws directed at rural people have their consent, and (5) address the real problems of the countryside that are destroying its communities, its culture, and its children's future. Is anyone listening?

12

ONTARIO FESTIVAL OF HUNTING CELEBRATES THE HOUND

2002

What is a book on hunting without at least one run with the beagles or bassets? Should a man or woman even be considered a true hunting person if he or she hasn't legged it for a few hours after a foot pack? After all, hunting on foot does provide another dimension to the sport and offers an entirely different perspective in the field.

Having come to hunting through a love of horses, I admit to being rarely seen hunting on foot. I recommend it, but in moderation.

Hounds from eight packs—foxhounds, beagles, and bassets—left their nose prints all over the hunting countries of Ontario from October 3 through 14, exuberantly trailing their appropriate quarries: coyote, fox, hare, and cottontail. More than two hundred hunting enthusiasts representing nineteen hunts from as far south as Tennessee, Georgia, and South Carolina enjoyed the unique camaraderie of the field as they followed hounds on horseback and on foot, all the while consuming great quantities of food and drink provided by their hospitable Canadian hosts in what was described as the biggest and most successful Ontario hunting festival ever.

Mounted foxhunters enjoyed six days of sport in the hunting countries of the Eglinton and Caledon, Hamilton, London, Toronto and North York, and the Wellington Waterloo. Guest foxhound packs came from the Hillsboro (TN), the Rose Tree (PA), and the Stone Valley (NY). Foot followers were shown exceptional sport by the Hidden Meadow Beagles (PA), the Calf Pasture Bassets (MD), and the Orange County Hare Hounds (VT).

With the weather unseasonably hot and dry, hounds struggled through the early days of the festival. Compounding the problem was a shortage of quarry.

"We've had a terrible mange problem here," said Mark Powell, huntsman of the Toronto and North York. "The coyotes have been wiped out."

A DAY ON FOOT

In nature, of course, one man's meat is another man's poison. With a shortage of coyote and fox, the hare and cottontail are thriving. By Friday, October 11, rain and fog finally replaced the brilliant sunshine, and one hundred sportsmen and women arrived at the new Toronto and North York kennels to follow the bassets. They were treated to a fabulous day of sport.

On the very first draw, a large European hare leapt out of the grass in view of the field and bounded away in an impressive burst of speed. These hare have beautiful tawny bodies and black-tipped ears. The bassets tore after it, throwing their magnificent, resonant bassos and pushing the hare hard. With the quarry heading toward the only road in this big, open country, Mark Powell, the sole mounted staff member, galloped hard and stopped the pack. Master Jeep Cochran of the Calf Pasture and Master Laura Janney of the Orange County collected hounds and set out again, showing the large field excellent sport all day.

"The big difference I notice between foot-hunting and mounted hunting is that everyone here is smiling," observed my walking companion. "Perhaps foxhunters spend too much time worrying about their horses!"

Drawing back toward the meet several hours later with a well-satisfied (and hungry) field behind, the bassets began hunting back

Jody Murtagh, MFH of the Rose Tree Foxhunting Club in Pennsylvania, was invited to bring his Penn-Marydel foxhounds to the Ontario Festival of Hunting. They proved to be a novelty to the Canadians who at the time hunted mostly English foxhounds. *Jim Meads photo*

toward the field. For a good twenty minutes they searched intently, speaking confidently and urgently in fits and starts. Slowly they worked their way toward us, breasting a small hill, covering every inch of it, speaking and affirming their confidence in the outcome. The unseen hare held tight all through the commotion until he knew the game was up. He leapt out of the grass not five feet from the lead hound and flew away in a straight dash across two fields—a distance of about a mile. Short legs notwithstanding, the bassets proved they really *can* run.

A DAY ON HORSEBACK

Speaking of great voices, Canadian sportsmen as well as some Americans had their chance to hunt behind Penn-Marydel foxhounds for the first time. Reactions were interesting to observe. "What are they doing?" was the oft-asked question, as the Penn-Marydels cold-trailed their quarry, throwing their voices enthusiastically in situations where the English or Crossbred hound wouldn't even deign to speak. Each time their full, deep voices trumpeted from the covert, the hands of the Field Master and the thrusters would creep up the reins, expecting to be in full gallop momentarily, only to find they had walked another twenty feet.

"We've been on this run for thirty minutes," said one, as he walked along on the buckle.

"Time for second horses," quipped another.

Those were the last wisecracks heard. Moments later, the pack exploded out of covert. The Field Master cocked an ear, wheeled his horse around, and we found ourselves back on a gravel road which we pelted down, fast and straight for two miles. We could hear hounds running ahead of us, and any prejudices about the Penn-Marydel's lack of foot were laid to rest right there. Hounds gave us another fast run on a red fox before the Masters called it a day. We returned to the meet to find yet another delicious hunt breakfast awaiting us.

THE NIAGARA ESCARPMENT*

The hunting country of the Toronto and North York and the Eglinton and Caledon is a product of and is situated in the lee of the famous Niagara Escarpment. It is an intriguing mix of spacious, open, flattish farmland and an equally spacious rolling country of small hills that fold one into the other. There are pasture lands for grazing cattle, but the soil is devoted primarily to crops—beans, corn, and that famous Canadian hay. Superb horses are raised in this limestone country.

---

* Escarpment: *Long steep slope at the edge of a plateau* (Oxford Dictionary). The Niagara Escarpment is a high ridge of limestone dolomite left behind by the glacial rivers that eroded the softer, looser materials along its eastern edge hundreds of millions of years ago. It runs along the western shore of Georgian Bay from the bay's northernmost point, southward past the Ontario hunting countries, and ends at Niagara Falls. The waters of the falls tumble over the escarpment's end.

Organizing six days of hunting for eight packs of hounds in five different hunting countries for over two hundred people working up huge appetites and great thirsts had to be an immense challenge. Walter Pady, MFH of the Toronto and North York, organized the foxhunting, while Jane Pady, ex-MFH, organized the foot hunting. The glue keeping the entire production synchronized and operating was provided by Festival Secretary Judy Jones.

Honorary Patron Henry Hooker, MFH of the Hillsboro Hounds, kicked the festival off to a rollicking start by dissolving his audiences in laughter whenever he spoke. Events were well recorded by Jim Meads, honorary photographer, who came from England and legged it across the hunting terrain in his familiar green slicker to get to all the right places at the right time.

In a brief welcoming speech at a party recognizing the Montreal Hunt as the oldest hunt in North America (176 years), Walter Pady noted the extraordinary camaraderie between all the participants. "How privileged we are to be able to sit on a horse and follow these packs of well-bred foxhounds, in a very special hunting country, seeing old friends, and making new friends," he said.

13

'WARE ARMADILLO

2002

It was early 1994 and snowing a blizzard in Virginia the first time I met Marty Wood, MFH of the Live Oak Hounds (FL). Marty, who was the outgoing president of the MFHA, and Jimmy Young, MFH of the Orange County Hunt (VA), who was the incoming president, were interviewing candidates to take over management of the MFHA office from John Glass, who was retiring. I had thrown my hat into the ring, but I had ulterior motives.

The snow was probably six inches deep when I arrived. Normally, I wouldn't have ventured out in my vehicle in such horrible conditions, but since the idea of an interview is to make a favorable impression, I took it as an opportunity to appear heroic. Jimmy already knew why I was there because I had broached my idea to him at a Virginia Foxhound Club luncheon on an earlier occasion; he and I were on the same page. After the preliminary greetings and introductions, Marty led off.

"Considering all the things you have done in your career, why do you want this job?" he asked.

"Well, I really don't want this job," I answered. "What I really would like to do is publish a newsletter about foxhunting for the MFHA. There are thousands of foxhunters out there—just members of the field like me—that love this sport, but no one talks to them. The MFHA should be the voice of foxhunting in North America."

Fortunately for all concerned, Lt. Col. Dennis Foster was hired as executive director of the MFHA. And after making my proposal to the MFHA board meeting in May, I got to start Covertside *with funding from the MFHA Educational Foundation chaired by Marty.*

Although Marty no longer hunts the Live Oak hounds himself, as he did when this story was written, he remains one of the world's most respected breeders of foxhounds, and it was an honor to be invited to hunt behind his brilliant pack.

White puffs of cotton left scattered over the bare ground by the harvester flew beneath us as we hammered across the stubble trying to keep on terms with the electrifying music of hounds. The Live Oak pack of Crossbred and English foxhounds were pushing their quarry—a gray fox—in a do-or-die straight-necked dash for his home country.

They had found their fox after his night's courting in a large pine plantation. For more than thirty minutes hounds had struggled through the dense undergrowth on the tortuous and twisting line of this most evasive quarry before finally pushing him into the open. Astonishingly, eight hounds—almost twenty percent of the pack fielded by the Live Oak Masters this day—have been champions at the Virginia Foxhound Show, America's foremost hound show.

I had driven more than eight hundred miles south from my Virginia home to Monticello, Florida, for a day with the Live Oak Hounds, and rain had been the unanimous prediction of every forecaster for Saturday, the day of the meet. You have to understand that rain in Florida often produces not simply the annoying moist collar, shoulders, and thighs to which most of us are accustomed. Rain in Florida is often a deluge, where three inches can fall in twenty minutes. When it's over, you might as well have been submerged in a lake. I've been caught out hunting when one of these came through, but I was younger and more tolerant then.

Daphne Wood, Joint-Master of the Live Oak, had promised to put me up on Riley, an eighteen-hand Irish Draft–Thoroughbred cross on which one crosses the country as comfortably and as safely as sitting in a deep, plush sofa. Fences? The same steady, effortless rhythm. He does it all himself—even fools you into believing you can ride a little. When you follow hounds on Riley, you're just a passenger with time for

With Master and huntsman Marty Wood recuperating from back surgery, Charles Montgomery hunted the Live Oak hounds this day. Twenty percent of the hounds fielded had been champions at the Virginia Foxhound Show, America's foremost hound show.   *Joan Fine photo*

watching hounds work and for gawking at a few of the more than one hundred fifty thousand acres of prime quail-shooting and working farm country over which the Live Oak hounds hunt. I had ridden Riley just a year ago—one week before visiting Olympic gold medalist Captain Mark Phillips rode him. I like to think I gave Riley a good school for the captain, even though I never did receive a note of acknowledgment.

"I'm sorry," said Daphne the night before the meet over a supper of wild turkey and sausage. "A two-hour race after 'the coyote from hell' last week, and Riley came up lame. We all ran out of horse on that one. I'm going to put you on Fitz tomorrow. He's just a first-year horse, but a wonderful hunter."

Oh, boy, I thought. There goes my deep, plush sofa! Then,

immediately, I was ashamed for thinking of myself first when this mar-velous horse was unwell. (I subsequently heard that Riley recovered completely and a few weeks later carried Captain Mark Phillips once again across the Live Oak country. I hope he went well for the captain, even though I didn't get a chance to school him first.)

Early the next morning I drove to the Live Oak stables to put my stirrups and leathers on Fitz's saddle. I was greeted by Piper Parrish and Kathy Barnett, second whippers-in, who work together like a well-oiled machine making hunters and turning them out for the Masters and huntsman. Fitz, tacked and ready to travel, turned out to be a gorgeous bay gelding. Pretty is as pretty does, I reminded myself. A first-year horse. Oh, boy.

I followed the horse trailer to the meet, which was fixtured for Copper's Field. As we approached, I was delighted to spy an armadillo scurrying across a bare cotton field. These prehistoric creatures are numerous in the south, but are not highly regarded by foxhunters. Like woodchucks in the more northern climes, armadillos riddle the hunting country with their holes, a danger to horses and riders.

After greeting a few familiar faces at the meet whom I remembered from last year's visit, I mounted Fitz. My wife Joan swept the horse with a practiced eye.

"Nice," she pronounced. "He looks like a show hunter."

Pretty is as pretty does, I reminded myself again.

Charles Montgomery was hunting hounds this day, because Master and huntsman Marty Wood was recovering from back surgery. Post-surgery restrictions notwithstanding, Marty was there in his vehicle, driving not only the vehicle but also Daphne to distraction by neglecting his doctor's instructions. The meet was in cotton farming country ad-jacent to a large, thickly wooded covert holding a tight undergrowth of ty-ty bushes, cat claw briars, and honeysuckle into which Montgomery sent the hounds. Legitimate quarry for most of the southern packs in this sort of country are coyote, red fox, gray fox, and bobcat.

I eagerly accepted Field Master Mercer Fearington's invitation to ride up, and we followed huntsman and hounds into the woods. Very soon a hound's voice rang out from the depths of the undergrowth. A pause, then another. The strike hounds worked up to their quarry steadily, deliberately. More hounds acknowledged the find and sang out in agreement, and soon the cold line turned into a warm track that gave every indication of being the drag of a gray fox. I was delighted.

We have virtually no gray fox in the part of Virginia where I hunt, and I know that this cunning creature and a good pack of hounds can produce a textbook demonstration of venery at its loftiest level. Neat wide rides cut through the thicket at intervals allowed staff and field to stay with hounds as they worked out the line. Indeed, the gray, loath to leave the covert, was living up to his reputation for twists, turns, jinks, and double-backs.

The Live Oak hunting country is vast and uninhabited, with few roads to worry the huntsman. What roads there are are mostly unpaved clay, with deep drainage ditches cut along both sides. Fitz jumped the first ditch confidently and cleanly; I could feel his back roll up under me. The rain hadn't materialized, and Fitz was proving himself to be a pure pleasure.

Hounds persevered, and for over thirty minutes we galloped through the woods, careening around right-angle corners where the rides intersected. I was amazed at the speed at which the horses in front of me took the corners. After skidding around the first, I decided I had better start giving Fitz some support with my leg. The hound music was thrilling. I lost track of the number of times we circled and reversed. And then, suddenly, there were two symphonies playing independently. A brace of foxes and a split.

We burst out of the woods into a field with perhaps ten couple of hounds absolutely tied to their line. The remainder of the pack, deep in the woods, sang to their own line. Montgomery, always in close touch with hounds, is a quiet and sympathetic huntsman, interfering very little, but quickly decisive when necessary. He called only once and our ten couple lifted their heads in unison and flew to him. He whirled about and sent them on to the others.

"That's English biddability," said Daphne.

With the pack back together the pressure in the covert became too intense for the hunted fox, and he finally broke. He made a straight-necked dash for his home country, but hounds were settled to his line. I followed Field Master Fearington over a coop—Fitz jumping confidently like a seasoned hunter—out of the woodland and into the open farm country. The music swelled from the entire pack, inspiring Fitz and me to a single-minded partnership determined to keep up. We flew across the cotton fields for another fifteen exhilarating minutes until the fox tried to go to ground in a stick pile and was caught by hounds.

This splendid pack had put on a hunting clinic—cold trailing, turning with their fox, driving him into the open, and finally accounting for him—with style and keen responsiveness to their huntsman. Before the day was over, hounds had found another gray and, with the same polish and panache, put it to ground.

I have not seen a more level pack of hounds in this country than the Live Oak. Whether full English or Crossbred, they are all of a type, leaning toward the modern English look—active, racy, and elegant. In most cases, it's hard to tell the English from the Crossbreds.

Marty Wood, their breeder, was a devoted protégé, disciple, and friend of the late Captain Wallace, and the English bloodlines in the Live Oak kennels derive predominantly from the Exmoor going back to Wallace's old Heythrop lines.

"Ronnie sent me stallion hounds and bitches and told me to breed them to my Crossbreds," said Marty. "Then I breed those offspring back to the English."

Duke of Beaufort's and College Valley bloodlines are also prominent at Live Oak.

"The modern English foxhound *is* a crossbred," Marty pointed out, referring to the Welsh, Fell, and American bloodlines that were introduced into the old English stock by the great breeders of the twentieth century: Isaac Bell, the tenth Duke of Beaufort, Peter Farquhar, Newton Rycroft, and Ronnie Wallace. "Our hounds are just the crossbred side of the modern English hound."

Marty is widely recognized as one of the hunting world's foremost judges of foxhounds. He and Daphne have judged every hound show in the United States, including the major shows in England. Last year, Marty had the singular honor of becoming the first American to judge foxhounds at the Royal Peterborough Foxhound Show.

The Live Oak kennels, separated from the hunt stables by a stately grove of loblolly pines and live oaks, are architecturally beautiful as well as functionally spacious and airy. Marty and Daphne have been the sole Masters for all of Live Oak's twenty-eight years. With that period of breeding continuity it's not surprising that the Live Oak hounds are among the finest in this country—in the field *and* on the flags.

14

CLOSE ENCOUNTER

2003

When Mason Houghland—in his 1933 gem of a book, Gone Away—*referred to the "sweet spice of danger" as one of the attractions of foxhunting, he was undoubtedly referring to the accidents that occasionally befall man and horse while crossing the country. I doubt if this one ever crossed his mind.*

The cornfield lay quiet, the stalks yellow and dry in the slant of the early morning October light. A section of the field had already been harvested and, arriving early, we parked in the neatly cut stubble, next to the hound trailer and staff horses. As the minutes ticked more vehicles and horse trailers arrived, an irregular procession nosing their way onto the stubble forming reasonably neat rows. People disembarked, swapped jackets for riding coats, pulled on boots, fussed with their horses, and struck up the usual cheerful premeet chatter. It was still cubhunting season, and the huntsman liked to draw the uncut cornfields to give the young entry a good school in using their noses. No one gave the cornfield a second glance.

Blue Ridge huntsman Dennis Downing approached and asked, "Does anyone have an extra necktie? I left mine home." No one seemed to have an extra, so I removed mine and gave it to him. He thanked me, slid it under his collar, and while knotting it, turned to the Master, Linda Armbrust, so they could discuss the draws of the day. The cornfield was first, and Downing asked that the field be sent down to hold up the far end so the fox and hounds wouldn't run toward Route 7. We followed first whipper-in Sue Downing, Dennis's wife, and spread out along the corn to slap our boots and chirp at the unseen quarry. In this circumstance, chatter is helpful and field members made the most of their opportunity. We saw nothing, heard nothing.

The first sign something was up was the approaching sound of a horse and rider at a gallop. This was no rhythmic hand gallop; it was flat out, the sound of a horse pounding toward us as fast as its rider could push it. It turned out to be Dennis Downing's daughter Emma, riding as second whipper-in. She streaked by us in a blur, eyes forward, obviously on a mission.

We jogged back to where we had last seen the huntsman, and found him tending to an injured hound and using his horn to call the rest of the hounds in. His story was a whopper:

Dennis had sent hounds into the corn, and they quickly opened. The cry was so intense that he thought it might be a coyote, quarry rarely seen in our hunting country. He was even more convinced it was coyote when he heard the unmistakable noises of struggle. If hounds had caught a fox, there would be no struggle. Downing dismounted and walked into the corn trying to follow the sounds as he rustled his way through the uncut corn stalks. He saw a flash of black. A black coyote?

There was little visibility in the corn, and it wasn't until Downing had pushed his way very close when he was stunned to see a fully grown black bear running directly toward him, pursued by hounds. "It was jet black with a glossy coat—obviously in good condition," recalled Downing.

The bear, which we can assume to have been in a distinctly poor humor, brushed Downing's leg as it ran past. Hounds followed in a frenzy. Just past Downing, the bear turned and grabbed the closest hound.

"The bear pinned it to the ground, clawed at it, then grabbed it round the neck in his mouth and shook it like a terrier would shake

Blue Ridge huntsman Dennis Downing and hounds early in the cubhunting season. Downing is wearing his own tie in this photo. *Karen L. Myers photo*

a rat," said Downing. "Other hounds were around him, baying at him. I waved my whip and shouted at the top of my lungs, mainly to get hounds away."

Emma Downing saw the bear leave the corn, then go back in. Having skinned out a number of bears in the course of her taxidermy work, she estimated its weight at two hundred fifty to three hundred pounds. Using his whip, voice, and horn, Downing got the hounds to follow him out of the corn. It was at that point in his adventure that we showed up.

An examination of the hounds showed several with cuts and bruises, but only two were in need of immediate medical attention. Bargain, an Orange County–bred bitch, had her throat ripped open and a cantaloupe-size hematoma from internal bleeding. Attic, a Crossbred hound, had no visible wounds, but was obviously in great pain. Both were in shock, but, miraculously, both are recovering well now. The hound that Downing had seen the bear pin to the ground and shake came out of it without any visible wounds, just bruises and soreness.

On the phone a couple of days later, Downing mused about what he might expect when he takes Bargain and Attic back hunting. "They'll probably stick to my horse's legs for a while," he predicted.

"Damn, Dennis," I complained. "You could have really messed up my necktie."

15

THE LIVE OAK HOUNDS

Performance and *Beauty*

2003

The MFHA holds three directors meetings each year. The first is traditionally held in New York City (though that tradition was broken finally in 2010) the day before the annual meeting, which occurs on the last Friday in January; the second is held at Morven Park in Leesburg, Virginia, just before the Memorial Day weekend in late May on the occasion of the Virginia Foxhound Show; and the third, which takes place in October, is a floater held in the hunting country of whichever MFHA officer or director is courageous enough to stand up and invite the group. Since the October meeting is a work/play weekend for the board—meetings and hunting—the pressure is on to show good sport to an exceptionally discerning field. In 2003 Marty and Daphne Wood, MFHs of the Live Oak Hounds in Monticello, Florida, hosted the October board meeting.

Imagine you are Master and huntsman of a pack of foxhounds, and you are expecting two dozen visiting Masters and foxhound breeders from all over North America for a day's sport with your hounds. No problem, except . . . oh-oh . . . no rain for three weeks and the forecasts are calling for soaring temperatures. Maybe there won't be any scent. You begin to imagine drawing coverts blank, hounds mutely following your horse, and what in the world are you going to do with all these Masters breathing down your neck hour after hour?

Surely some of these thoughts chilled the minds of Marty and Daphne Wood as they spent the final few days preparing to host the fall directors meeting of the MFHA at Live Oak in Monticello, Florida, for the second time in ten years. (The first was during Marty's tenure as MFHA president; this, the second, during Daphne's.) The visiting Masters had been invited to join the hunt's subscribers on Sunday, October 26, for the thirtieth-anniversary Opening Meet of the Live Oak Hounds.

Perhaps Marty had no doubts at all. He knows better than anyone the passion, attention, determination, and resources he has invested for thirty years in the breeding of what has become recognized as one of the finest packs of foxhounds in the country. On the eve of the meet, as a final step to insure the best possible sport, he has moved the meeting time back to seven a.m. to take advantage of the cooler—if you call sixty-seven degrees cool—early morning temperatures. He is prepared. What could possibly go wrong?

Morning dawns. The twenty-six and a half couples drafted for the day's work are bouncing about in the holding yard watching the usual premeet bustle of arriving trailers and followers. Thirty minutes to "show time."

Sprong! An eager hound has leapt up and somehow released the latch on the holding yard door. Breakout! The entire pack bursts through the freely swinging gate and races off at a pace that suggests, "Don't wait supper; we may be home late." Fortunately, biddability is a hallmark of the Live Oak pack, and despite the exuberance of their initial burst, the truants are quickly stopped and collected. What can go wrong, indeed. And it isn't yet seven o'clock.

By seven, the pack of English and mostly seven-eighths English Cross-breds were trotting sedately by Master Wood's horse on their way to the first draw. With the false start behind him, Marty Wood and his hounds proceeded to give a clinic on how to hunt the fox.

The fox spied the renowned photographer Jim Meads and decided to immortalize himself.
Jim Meads photo

Finding immediately, hounds slowly and persistently worked up to their fox with great cry, got it to its feet, and pushed it relentlessly and musically for forty minutes through all his circles, jinks, and double-backs. With but a few checks, hounds pressured their quarry out of covert finally and into a large hayfield at Live Oak, bisected by the driveway and bordered by the county road. Finding a large and appreciative audience in the hayfield, this handsome red-sided gray proceeded to put on a show of its own.

The fox ran past the first field of visiting Masters and directors; headed for the second, larger field of faithful followers, giving them their own closeup; spied the well-known English sporting photographer Jim Meads, and decided to immortalize himself by heading for Meads's famous lens and streaking past no more than twenty feet away; and, with a final burst of energy (which was clearly flagging), was sportsman enough to run the gauntlet of car followers, foot followers, and any other individual lucky enough to be driving by at the time.

This was the finest view of a hunted fox in terms of the size of the audience privileged to view him that this reporter has ever witnessed.

While Charles James was putting on his show, hounds burst into
the open behind him. Just as they passed me the first two hounds
lifted their noses from the ground, caught sight of their quarry, shifted
gear, and coursed him across the field. In the lead was Trooper 2000,
Champion Entered Crossbred dog hound at the Mid-America Hound
Show. Trooper's littermate, Trusty 2000, Champion Crossbred bitch
at the same show, ran a close third. Both were sired by a son of Live
Oak Drummer 1989, two-time champion dog hound at Virginia.

Tiring and losing ground with every stride, the fox managed to
dive into covert and save his brush by going to ground. It was a magnificent hound hunt to the end, with tremendous cry from the entire
pack, prompting Marty to say, with his tongue planted firmly in his
cheek, "Too bad English hounds have no voice!"

Time and again the Live Oak pack demonstrates its biddability. At one
check, most of the pack was outside the covert, hunting along the edge
when a lone hound spoke from a hundred-fifty yards distant. Marty
tipped his horn toward the speaking hound, called once, and every
hound lifted its head in unison, abandoned its hunt, and harked to the
speaking hound.

Marty uses his horn and his voice while drawing to keep in touch
with hounds, but once they find and start hunting, he leaves them
alone. We were in a field when hounds checked. The fox had been
seen, several caps were aloft, and a *tally-ho* was heard from the other
side of a small covert. Wood sat motionless on his horse and did nothing. I turned to Jody Murtagh, MFH and huntsman of the Rose Tree
(PA), one of the visiting directors.

"That must be the hardest thing for a huntsman to do," I whis-
pered. "Nothing."

"Yes, it is hard," replied Murtagh, "but it's also a measure of how
much a huntsman trusts his hounds."

Marty remained silent, the staff was motionless and quiet, then a hound spoke, then another, and the pack was on again. After the hunt, I asked Marty the same question and received the same answer almost verbatim.

"I trust my hounds," said Marty. "I can't hunt the fox, so I have to trust them to do it."

Despite the rising temperature, the day ended with another superb hunt on a bobcat, which hounds accounted for.

Of the twenty-six and a half couple of hounds in the field this day, *five couple* have been champions at major hound shows. Arguably Live Oak is one of the very few packs of foxhounds in North America able to hunt with such intensity and style *and* compete in the show ring with such domination. To hunt with this pack is to experience first-hand a superior standard of performance and beauty.

16

THE GREATER GIFT

2004

Five years have passed since this story was published—an eternity to a ten-year-old. My young friend, Denya Dee Leake, now an accomplished foxhunter, is often recruited to ride with Blue Ridge Hunt's first whipper-in Sue Downing. This brings her enjoyment and education to a new level entirely.

That she is an elegant and capable horsewoman is no surprise. Her mother, Caroline Treviranus Leake, rode for the United States in two Three-Day World Championships in the 1970s; her late grandfather Stuart Treviranus rode for the Canadian Three-Day Team; her grandmother Marilyn Mackay-Smith hunted in her native Ontario, in Virginia, and whipped-in at Blue Ridge in her day; and her late step-grandfather, Alexander Mackay-Smith, ex-MFH, was my mentor in foxhunting history and literature. What goes around comes around.

This season, on school holidays and Saturdays, I have been taking a ten-year-old girl, a close friend of the family, foxhunting. When we return, her mother thanks me for taking her. Her grandmother thanks me, too. Yet *I* have received a greater gift. After forty years following hounds, I have been given the opportunity to see foxhunting anew, through fresh eyes.

My young friend is like a sponge. Her eyes and ears are wide open, and she wants to know everything. Most of all, of course, she wants to gallop and jump. But she has been learning the difficult lessons of patience as well, especially at the start of cubhunting.

At the Blue Ridge Hunt, we "do" the cornfields for the first few weeks. The Masters use members of the field to "hold up" the coverts, so the young entry can learn what this game is all about. It can be tedious duty, and my friend did get restless at times. But cubhunting is also a wonderful opportunity to tune in to what huntsman and hounds are doing.

"What's she saying?" my young friend asked. (Huntsman Dennis Downing's daughter Emma was hunting hounds that day while his broken wrist was healing.) My friend's question made me reflect for a moment on the arcane and often incomprehensible noises the huntsman uses to communicate to his hounds. How baffling that must be to the uninitiated.

"If you listen carefully," I replied, "you'll hear her say, 'Lieu in, lieu in. . . .' She is telling the hounds to get on into the covert and look for a fox."

Later, I overheard a replay of my very words as my friend recounted her day's hunting to her chum. Like a sponge. I was opening her eyes to something she will hopefully enjoy for a very long time. Longer than I will ever know.

Moving on from the cornfield, finally, I gave my friend a choice: the coop or the gate? She opted for the gate. Later, waiting on the road at our Knightsbridge covert, I knew that if hounds found, the only way in was via a coop. I kept mum. Hounds found, and I turned to her. "Get right behind me; there's just a *little* coop in here." After jumping it, I turned to see her sail over. When hounds checked and we pulled up, she was beaming.

"My first coop!" she gushed.

The next Saturday, as we approached the first coop, she asked, in an effort to reassure herself, "It's just a *small* one, isn't it?"

"Yes," I said.

Confidence was building. How did I know? After that one, I found her galloping in front of me and giving me a lead over the next coop. I decided I'd better regain control. I arched an eyebrow and pointed behind me. She got it.

By taking my young friend Denya Dee Leake hunting every Saturday, I received a gift—the opportunity to see foxhunting anew, through fresh eyes. She was like a sponge. Her eyes and ears were wide open, and she wanted to know everything. *Gamecock photo*

For the last couple of hunts, my friend has ridden behind me in the first flight over every obstacle on some great runs. When she sees the huntsman with his hounds gliding up the valley or the pack sweeping in an arc as one, singing and tied to the line, she now directs *my* attention to the scene. With eyes like saucers, she asks rhetorically, "Isn't that beautiful?"

There were only a handful of diehards left with hounds as we headed back to the meet the last time out. The Master, Linda Armbrust, turned to her and said, "Denya Dee, come up front here with me." I hacked along contentedly behind. My friend's back was straight and proud. Imagine how I felt.

EPILOGUE

A conversation with my creative friend author/editor Steven Price about my experiences in the hunting field with Denya Dee led to the creation of *Covertside's* "Mac & DeDe" series. The idea was to teach youngsters coming to the sport a different hunting concept in each issue, hopefully in a light way. The cartoon shown here ran in the Fall 2008 issue.

Mac & DeDe
Norman Fine and Jean Abernethy

WHAT WE NEED NOW IS FOR THE HUNTSMAN TO MAKE A BRILLIANT CAST.

HOW CAN HE DO THAT? HE DIDN'T EVEN BRING A ROD.

Mac is not telling DeDe a fish story. When hounds are *at fault* (have lost the scent they were following), they often make an organized sweep of the area in a large arc—either on their own or guided by the huntsman—in an attempt to recover the line. This is a *cast*.

The huntsman will usually allow hounds to *cast* themselves first. It's their job to find and follow the fox, and he doesn't want to interfere too quickly. He wants a good work ethic in his pack, and he doesn't want them looking to him every time they have a problem. However, the longer it takes for hounds to recover the line, the more distance the fox is putting between himself and the hounds, and the weaker the scent becomes.

Having given hounds a chance to recover the line themselves, the huntsman may decide to help by collecting hounds and making his own *cast*. The most common is the "round the hat" *cast*, where the huntsman leads hounds in a large circle around the area where they lost, making certain he brings them a distance back of that point just in case the fox doubled back on its line.

And here is where a huntsman may show his genius. He may *cast* hounds toward a faraway covert or a large earth he knows of, suspecting that the fox may have likely headed that way. Or he may recall a similar run several seasons back, where the fox made an unexpected turn through a nearby barnyard of cattle and *foil* (confusing smells), and he might *cast* them in that direction.

Mac is watching and hoping for his huntsman to make an inspired *cast*!

17

HUNTING WITH THE CORNWALL HOUNDS

2004

I had met Tony Leahy when he was a director of the MFHA and hunted with him several times when he was the designated huntsman for many of the fox-hound performance trials. While serving as a director, Tony implemented the innovative Professional Development Program for the MFHA, which enrolls a handful of selected young professional staff members each year into a structured program of education and mentoring.

Tony is a nephew of the legendary Willie Leahy, former Field Master of the County Galway—the Blazers—in Ireland. In addition to his devotion to foxhunting, he had an open jumping career in Ireland and England before coming to the States.

I love to hunt with Tony because, in addition to his obvious talents as a huntsman, he is probably one of the most beautiful riders you will ever see crossing the country. As he canters by, I imagine my legs to be a few inches longer, my heels a couple of inches lower, my back a tad straighter. I could ride like that, too, I dream.

Before settling down to the business of their annual fall directors meeting, visiting MFHA officers and directors had a day's hunting with the Cornwall Hounds in Stockton, Illinois. Tony Leahy, MFH and huntsman of both the Cornwall Hounds and the Fox River Valley Hunt, hunts three times a week, alternately in the Cornwall and Fox River Valley countries until winter shuts him down. Then he picks up hounds and takes them to Georgia, where they continue the season through March.

Leahy's Cornwall country is about two and a half hours west of Chicago's O'Hare Airport and about twenty miles, as the crow flies, east of the Mississippi River, which is the Iowa border. Here Leahy hunts the coyote over more than *one hundred thousand acres* of what was, until now, hunting's best-kept secret. The directors that came to hunt will tell you that it is probably the most beautiful and perfect country for hunting the fox or coyote that we have in North America.

The terrain is reminiscent of the English hunting country, but on a larger scale. The hills aren't steep, but they're big, and they roll gently and randomly, fold upon fold, to the horizon. From the hilltops, the vistas open up for fifty miles or more, with virtually nothing but large-acreage farmland between you and the farthest hill. The coverts are small, and the large fields that haven't been planted in corn or soybeans are in natural grass or pasture. In fact, many of the farmers are removing acreage from cultivation, with the encouragement and assistance of the federal government, and placing it into the Conservation Resource Program (CRP). Many of these uncultivated fields are being replanted, again with federal help, with the old, native prairie grasses.

Both beef and dairy cattle thrive, and the rich green alfalfa fields provide bright accents to the dry-brown stretches of corn stubble and switch grass. As if this country isn't inviting enough, know that the foxhunter gallops carefree across fields that are free of holes, and when he does come across a road, it's paved in smooth, fine-grain gravel and sand!

Leahy's pack is seventy-five percent Crossbred, containing Midland and some pure July bloodlines, the other twenty-five percent being mostly English with ST-Carlow and North Warwickshire lines.

"People will tell you there's a bit of everything in the pack," Leahy says with a wry grin, "but we do have a plan!" Indeed, even the Walker with the curly stern and the black and tan hounds with the Scarteen bloodlines have been crossed with Leahy's Carlow and North Warwick-

Tony Leahy takes hounds to a view.   *Jake Carle photo*

shire lines. Leahy has been very pleased with his Scarteen crosses and rates them highly for hunting the coyote.

Now for the hunting. I don't know how many packs can account for a coyote in thirty-five minutes over open country, but Leahy's pack did.

"Tony just gave a textbook example of how to hunt the coyote," said Marty Wood, MFH of the Live Oak Hounds (FL). "He let his hounds settle on the line, and he let them hunt." Wood explained, "It's constant pressure that kills coyote. There were no long checks. Hounds really kept the pressure on. They pushed and pushed."

"Short, sharp, and decisive," exclaimed Mason Lampton, MFH of the Midland Fox Hounds (GA), quoting his father-in-law Ben Hardaway's mantra.

Hounds found in covert and, making a grand chorus, switched direction several times before pushing the coyote into the open. While still in covert, Leahy displayed great patience. He encouraged hounds from a distance, but made no effort either to get close to them or to follow every time they changed direction. When, finally, they did go away, he got with them and stayed with them. Seeing Leahy periodically, gliding effortlessly ahead as I scrambled and pushed to keep up, I was reminded of a line from Somerville and Ross: "Always ahead of me was Flurry Knox, going as a man goes who knows his country, who knows his horse, and whose heart is wholly and absolutely in the right place."

It was a fast, nonstop run for the field, later estimated to be a five-mile point. The footing was somewhat deep due to three inches of rain the day and night before—tiring for horses and hounds—but perfectly safe. Hounds accounted for their quarry in a small patch of covert in the bottomland where a three-foot vertical drop into a muddy streambed loosened me from my tack for a brief but perilous moment. Hounds went on to show more sport, but the first run was the highlight, and many field members, in consideration of their tired horses, slipped back into the second field for the remainder of the day, where they were privileged with some excellent views of the hunted coyotes.

18

THE BEAR CREEK HOUNDS ARE IN HIGH COTTON

2005

In the course of my travels for Covertside, *it occurred to me that readers might be interested in learning about some of the newer and lesser known hunts around the country: how they got started, what obstacles they had to overcome, who the driving forces were, and what prompted them to start a hunt in the first place. This was my first story about a new hunt.*

The good folks of *Handley Cross* knew they wanted foxhunting in their country. So when their own Captain Doleful placed an advertisement in search of a Master of Foxhounds, Surtees' immortal character John Jorrocks answered the call. Arriving amidst great fanfare, Jorrocks gave his famous sporting lecture to the villagers, explaining his hunting philosophies.

> 'Unting is the sport of kings, the image of war without its guilt, and only twenty-five percent of its danger! . . . The 'oss and the 'ound were made for each other, and nature threw in the Fox as the connectin' link between the two. . . . In the summer I loves him with all the hardour of affection, but when the hautumn comes, 'ow I glories in pursuin' of him. . . . And yet, it arn't that I loves the fox less, but that I loves the 'ound more.

The good folks of Dooly County, Georgia, didn't know they wanted foxhunting. However, they *were* willing to listen. So Bear Creek

125

MFH Hal Barry and his three-man board of founding members—Phil Beegle, Rene Latiolais, and Warner Ray—gave their own version of Jorrocks's sporting lecture to several of the county's leading farmers and business leaders after dinner at a local restaurant. As a result, the newest MFHA-member hunt to be elevated to Recognized status, the Bear Creek Hounds of Moreland, Georgia, was able to add six more hunting fixtures encompassing more than sixty thousand acres of prime, open hunting country in Dooly and Sumpter counties to their more wooded country around Moreland.

SOMETHING OF VALUE

The icing on the cake, however, is the fact that as happy as the Bear Creek members are to be able to hunt over this excellent new country, the residents of Dooly County are equally pleased with the arrangement. They show up on hunting days in cars, trucks, and ATVs. One farmer, Jim Shirah, has been coming out on his Tennessee Walker in a western saddle. He is so enthusiastic about the Bear Creek gang and the thrill of foxhunting that he has pledged to learn to ride in an English saddle this summer and come out in a black coat next season! I asked Shirah what his reaction was after he heard the Bear Creek presentation on foxhunting that first evening.

"We recognized that these folks were bringing something of value to our community," he replied with sincerity.

Dooly County, south of Macon, is in the heart of Georgia's cotton farming country. Many of the farms are ten thousand acres in size or more. There is little fencing, and individual fields over which hounds run can be as large as three hundred to eight hundred acres each. The coverts are mostly pine plantations, loblolly and such, that are planted in the areas not conducive to cotton growing. When the pines are small, before the undergrowth can be annually burned, the vines and scrub grow thickly between the young trees, providing excellent hunting habitat for coyotes and bobcats in search of mice and

Hal Barry lived the Atlanta city life for years, but once he discovered foxhunting he couldn't leave it alone. With Ben Hardaway's support and advice, the Bear Creek Hounds were organized in 2001, accepted for Registration by the MFHA in 2003, and elevated to Recognized status just two years later. Hal is pictured here with his wife, Linda.   *Jim Meads photo*

other small animals. The footing is excellent—a loamy-sandy mix that drains well and absorbs the shock of hooves.

The farmers are prosperous, and their farming methods are very sophisticated. As an example, their tractors carry Global Positioning Satellite (GPS) systems on board. With this equipment, they traverse their cotton fields according to a grid pattern, taking soil samples at numerous points. The samples are then analyzed and keyed to the specific GPS locations from which they were taken. The data are run through a computer program that then instructs the fertilizer spreader, as it crosses the fields, to adjust the mix for the precise nutrients needed at each specific location. This saves the farmer a great deal of money, since he spreads only what is needed of each nutrient, and it saves the environment from the runoff of excess fertilizer that cannot be absorbed by the soil.

"It's fantastic country," said Hal Barry, MFH of this private pack. "It has raised our sport to a whole new level!"

And what level is that? one might ask. Well, hounds have killed seven coyotes this season, and they hunt just two days a week at present. As Ben Hardaway, MFH of the Midland Fox Hounds (GA), told Barry after a weekend of joint meets in Dooly County, "Of the one hundred and seventy hunts in North America, you're one of about fifteen that can kill a coyote."

Bear Creek huntsman Guy Cooper agrees that the Dooly County country has improved the pack. "With hounds running across big, open fields, I can now see which hounds are doing the work, which was very difficult in our wooded country," he said.

THE BEGINNINGS

MFH Hal Barry grew up, one of three boys in a family of six children, in a small rural town in Iowa.

"I would have been a farmer if my father could have afforded more land," he said.

Instead, Barry went to college, took a summer job in construction as a carpenter, and got a taste for building. Eventually, he wound up in Atlanta developing commercial real estate. Today, the Barry Company is the buzz of Atlanta with Allen Plaza, a planned downtown mixed-use development including three high-rise office buildings and a hotel/residential condo tower.

Barry doesn't subscribe to the "build it and they will come" philosophy.

"We find the users first, then build what they need," he said.

He compares hunting for users to hunting for coyotes.

"It's the thrill of the chase in both cases," he said. "You lose some, and you account for some. I've fallen from horses, and I've fallen in business, and I've been able to pick myself back up from both. It's creative and thrilling, and it's what keeps me young."

Barry and his wife, Linda, lived the Atlanta city life for years, playing tennis and running, but in 1981 he began having problems with his hips, which curtailed both activities. Looking for something else to do, he set out to buy fifty acres out in the country and wound up buying six hundred. The couple began shooting and riding and received their first exposure to foxhunting in the mid-1980s. Linda hunted with both the Shakerag Hounds and the Midland Fox Hounds (GA), and Hal became intrigued by hunting, but from a distance.

In 1989 Barry had both hips replaced, took riding lessons, and six months later rode in his first hunt, in the first field, with the Midland Fox Hounds in their Fitzpatrick, Alabama, country.

"I'll never forget that day," he said. "The morning, the crispness in the air, the beauty of the land, the hounds, the scarlet coats. I can't remember hearing a hound speak, but the beauty of the thing got to me. I couldn't leave it alone."

Thus began a very special relationship with his mentor, Ben Hardaway. Barry opened country around his Moreland farm and got Hardaway to bring hounds and hunt the country. Because it was unknown country to Hardaway, Barry found himself riding with Hardaway as a guide.

"I didn't know anything about hounds and hound work, but riding in Ben's back pocket I now realize that I had experienced a lifetime opportunity that left me hopelessly addicted to the cry of hounds," Barry said.

His new interest in hounds led Barry to begin walking Midland puppies—as many as twenty to thirty puppies a year! He exercised them first on foot, then on horseback. He got himself a horn and schooled the puppies to come to the horn.

"It was more damn fun!" he said.

The next step was inevitable. Barry got some old hounds from Midland and began hunting them himself.

"I *hounded* Hardaway for more hounds," he said.

Sometimes they worked for him, and sometimes they didn't. He bred a bitch he had out of Midland Secret to a dog he had by Midland's Faraday-Hardaway line from England. He produced two litters from these two exceptional tail lines. Soon Barry had twenty-five to thirty hounds—a respectable farmer's pack—and he built a new kennel. The next time Midland came to hunt his country, Hardaway looked at the kennel and exclaimed, "Hal, I could put a hundred fifty hounds in there!"

Hardaway's Joint-Master, Mason Lampton, encouraged Barry also. "Go for it," Lampton said. "Get Registered. We've got to give you the territory back."

Then the injury. A horse went down with him, and Barry broke a vertebra in his back. Barry had already become conscious of a growing conflict between the needs of the hounds for regular routine and the needs of his business for time and attention. Between the injury and the conflict, Barry gave serious thought to giving up the hounds. Then MFHA Executive Director Dennis Foster came up with the solution.

Foster told Barry about a young Welshman, Guy Cooper, then hunting hounds in Canada, who had the desire and a wife who rode like the wind, and who wanted to relocate. Barry invited Cooper to Georgia for a meeting, and a week later they had an agreement. Some months later, in 2003, the Bear Creek Hounds were accepted by the MFHA as a Registered pack. In January 2005, the hunt was elevated to Recognized status.

Barry maintains an all-professional hunt staff, with Guy Cooper as huntsman, Cooper's wife, Heather, as first whipper-in, and Kelly Barrett as second whipper-in. Barry believes that much of the pack's success this year is due to the fact that they hunt just two days a week.

"We try to hunt twenty-two-and-a-half to twenty-five-and-a-half couple. This gives our entered hounds a chance to hunt twice a week and gives Guy and his staff the remaining five days a week to spend quality time schooling and exercising both entered hounds and puppies," Barry said.

In his determination to have a quality hunt, Barry has discovered a completely unexpected dimension to the experience.

"Mason told me that you don't just do this for yourself; you want to make it available," Barry said. "I had never thought of the giving involved in having a hunt, but we have provided sport, and we have made a lot of people very, very happy."

WELCOME TO DOOLY COUNTY

After riding out in the steady rain and raw wintry weather with Guy and Heather Cooper to exercise hounds in the morning, I accompanied Linda on the two-hour drive to Dooly County that afternoon. Hal, who had spent the morning in his office, met us at Henderson Village, a charming resort of old southern homes, many of them moved to the village, restored, and converted to guest homes. It is here that the Bear Creek members overnight for the Dooly County fixtures.

The proprietor of Henderson Village, Bernhard Schneider, became fascinated with America as a young boy in Germany in 1945 while watching Hollywood films played for the American officers billeted in his aunt's hotel during the occupation. Schneider grew up to establish a successful consumer electronics company in Munich, and he eventually bought property in Georgia and developed Henderson Village.

The village also boasts an excellent restaurant where the Bear Creek members, staff, and Barry's guests happily fortify themselves for the next morning's hunting. Tonight's dinner was the prelude to the last hunt of the season, a most successful season, and afterdinner speeches were in order.

Barry spoke of the many wonderful new friends they had made among the farmer-landowners in Dooly County: Billy Sanders, for one, who has earned the national designation, High Cotton, and is recognized as the largest cotton producer in the Southeast; Wayne West, for another, chairman of the county commissioners; Shannon Akin, cotton farmer; Jim Braxton, a farmer whose crop-dusting airstrip we passed while hunting on the following day; Jim Shirah, who pledges to hunt in an English saddle and a black coat next season; and Chuck Ellis, director of the Dooly County Farm Extension Services whose farm was to host the next day's meet.

Guy Cooper then gave a brief review of the season, proudly recalling the pack's first coyote kill on a day in which he took twenty-two-and-a-half couple of hounds out and twenty-two couple were there at the kill—quite an achievement.

I spoke to Chuck Ellis the next morning before mounting up, and he confirmed all I had heard about Dooly County's warm welcome to the hunt.

"We love having them here," he said. "They're fine people, and they have such a good time."

Indeed, later that morning as we hacked between coverts near the road, a tractor stopped. The farmer climbed down and walked up to Guy Cooper, who slid off his horse and introduced himself. The man pointed to his farm, which was just across the road.

"The gates are unlocked," he said. "You're welcome to go anywhere you like."

LIVING HIS DREAM

I was exquisitely mounted on a twenty-two-year-old Hanoverian mare. Leica was totally uncomplicated, loved her hunting, and would go anywhere with confidence. She was sound, fit, fast, and completely adjustable.

"She's a tough mare," said Julie McKee, her owner, who is currently filling in for the injured second whipper-in, Kelly Barrett. And talented. "My husband took her in two combined training events last summer, and she won both of them."*

Rene Latiolais served as Field Master and kept us close to hounds as they worked. Huntsman Guy Cooper drew the fixture in a serpentine pattern, generally westerly from the meet. Hounds were hardworking, active, and biddable. After feathering on various night lines, struggling to trail up to the quarry, they suddenly all came together at the edge of a swampy area with a great cry.

"It must have been a bobcat," Cooper said later. "If it had been coyote they would have sounded three times as loud!"

Unable to get through directly, we had a fast pipe-opening gallop around the swamp to where hounds ultimately lost at the road. With ground moist from the previous day's rain and temperatures in the forties, everyone expected good scenting. Such was not to be the case, however.

Hounds found next at a drainage ditch, speaking enthusiastically, but unable to carry the line on. With one hound speaking in a covert several hundred yards away, huntsman Cooper had a dilemma. He waited patiently for the pack to make something of their find, and when they couldn't, he lifted them and took them to the hound that was speaking. Unfortunately, that petered out as well, prompting Hal Barry to remark that the slow day was undoubtedly due to all their boasting the previous evening.

Shortly thereafter, Barry, out on point, viewed a bobcat. Cooper brought his hounds to the view, and they went away directly on the line with a good cry. Under difficult scenting conditions, however, the covert proved large enough for the bobcat to evade hounds without leaving, and hounds were once again frustrated.

Though not the day to end the season that Bear Creek might have hoped for, hounds certainly displayed good effort, working hard for

---

* Two years later, at the age of twenty-four, with owner Julie McKee aboard, Leica won the Southern District Qualifier and placed third in the national finals of the Centennial Field Hunter Championships held at Morven Park in Virginia.

their huntsman and finishing the season with a brilliant record of which Master, staff, and members can be proud.

There is no doubt that Hal Barry is having the time of his life. Truth be told, however, when he first proposed his plans to start a hunt on their farm, Linda Barry was not equally enthusiastic. She had to give up some of her privacy and some of her peace and quiet, but she is enjoying her hunting now, and, every so often, when Hal comes up, gives her a peck on the cheek and says, "Thank you, honey, for letting me live my dream," Linda knows she got it right.

19

ROSE TREE AND THE PENN-MARYDEL

A Time-Honored Partnership

2004

I have published the annual foxhunting calendar for the MFHA since 1998. In the 2005 calendar I used a charming photograph taken the previous summer at the Virginia Foxhound Show. It showed a thirteen-year-old girl in a white kennel coat lying on her belly in the grass next to a foxhound bitch that was rolling luxuriously to scratch her own back. The young girl, Codie Hayes—granddaughter of Rose Tree MFH and huntsman Jody Murtagh—had just shown Rose Tree Needy 2002 in the final class of the Penn-Marydel division and had walked out of the ring with the championship cup. That qualified Needy to compete in the final class of the day against the champions in the American, English, and Crossbred rings for the title of Grand Champion foxhound of the largest and most prestigious foxhound show in North America. Codie and Needy were relaxing for what was shortly to become a historic first.

Mr. C. Martin Wood III, MFH, had been selected to judge the Grand Championship class. Wood is recognized as one of the foremost judges of foxhounds in the world, having judged every major hound show in North America and England. After scrutinizing the champion foxhounds from the four rings from every angle, Wood stunned the crowd of onlookers by choosing Rose Tree Needy as the Grand Champion. Why was that a stunner? Because Wood didn't make his selection on the basis of today's beauty standard. He chose Needy over the other three as the foxhound that was the most perfect specimen of her breed and type.

Five years have passed since that day. Rose Tree Master Jody Murtagh and his family now live in Southern Pines, North Carolina, where he is huntsman of the Moore County Hounds. Codie, now eighteen years old, hunts the hounds when Murtagh cannot. Here is the story of my first hunt behind Murtagh and his Penn-Marydels.

It was one o'clock in the morning. I had fallen into bed tired and happy just two hours earlier after a very long day: four hours of superb hunting behind the Penn-Marydel foxhounds of the Rose Tree Foxhunting Club and a three-hour drive home from Pennsylvania. Yet here I was awake and reliving the day's sport: four foxes, two marked to ground, two wonderful views of our quarry, and a good twenty miles under the girth of a good horse—much of it long gallops over big, rolling corn and wheat fields, up and down steep ridges bisected by stream beds in the bottom. As I tossed, turned, and cogitated, one question begged an answer. Why do these gentle hounds with their excellent noses and booming voices provoke such controversy among hunting people?

Detractors of the Penn-Marydel will tell you that (1) they look funny; (2) they are slow; and (3) they lack drive. There may well be a kernel of truth to all those claims, but Penn-Marydel enthusiasts can turn each criticism into an attribute.

Beauty, as they say, is in the eye of the beholder. Proponents of the Penn-Marydel zealously guard, indeed breed for and cherish, the Penn-Marydel *look*: the long, luxurious ears; the domed head; the relaxed foot; the gentle, kind expression. Penn-Marydel fans may well acknowledge that the beauty standard for today's foxhound is the modern English (or Crossbred) hound with its swan neck, deep chest curving gracefully up to a trim waist, smoothly rolling muscles over the loins, and tight feet. Nevertheless, they adore the classic hound look of *their* hounds much as the bobbysoxers a half century ago swooned over a skinny boy named Frank Sinatra. No Charles Atlas was *he*.

As for the Penn-Marydel's speed, true again. They *are* slower than their English cousins. Does this mean they will produce a slower hunt? Not necessarily. With their slower, steadier speed and low-scenting powers they can turn more quickly and accurately with the evasive moves of the fox. This can result in fewer losses, shorter checks, more pressure on the fox, and a faster hunt overall. At any rate, the difference in their speed isn't enough to allow their followers time to dawdle. Huntsman, staff, and your reporter were mounted on Thoroughbred types, and we galloped to stay with hounds.

The term *drive* is interesting to explore. When running the fox in full cry, the Rose Tree Penn-Marydels were as enthusiastic as any hounds I have seen. At the earth, however, I have to admit they were not as aggressive in marking or digging as are many English or Cross-bred hounds in that situation. They ran with fervor and enthusiasm, but did not appear equally determined to dispatch their quarry. Their game and their religion seemed to be the line of the fox rather than the terminal outcome of the chase.

Codie Hayes, granddaughter of MFH and huntsman Jody Murtagh, showed Rose Tree Needy 2002 to the Grand Championship of the 2004 Virginia Foxhound Show. *Susan Edwards photo*

Even detractors of the Penn-Marydel do not argue their many exceptional qualities. First and foremost are nose and voice. The Penn-Marydel is renowned for its low-scenting powers and mighty, resonant voice. They will provide sport on poor scenting days when other hounds cannot, and a pack in full cry will swell the woodlands with their music. They are very biddable in the field, relatively easy to deer-proof, and highly unlikely to fight in the kennel.

ORIGINS

"The early settlers of Pennsylvania and Maryland imported from England the 'Southern Hound' in great numbers. These hounds were known for their great scenting powers and patience in pursuit of the line of their quarry. These same colonials crossed their hounds with Gascon strains from France to increase their nose and voice and to gain the characteristic color of blue tick and black and tan. This cross—the English Southern Hound to the French Gascon strains— was the genesis of the Penn-Marydel foxhound" (*Covertside*, March 1997, Robert Crompton, MFH, Andrews Bridge Foxhounds).

In 1934, the name, Penn-Marydel, was formally established to represent that strain of American foxhound that had, for generations, been bred and hunted by sportsmen and women in the southeastern regions of Pennsylvania, Maryland, and Delaware. In that year, M. Roy Jackson, with the assistance of Mrs. Jackson, Walter Jeffords, William Ashton, and John B. Hannum, formed the Penn-Marydel Foxhounds, Inc., to "preserve purity in the bloodlines of a species of the American Foxhound which has been found to be most serviceable and satisfactory for club and pack hunting." Jackson was MFH of the Radnor Hunt and ex-MFH of the Rose Tree Foxhunting Club of Philadelphia, the oldest (1859) subscription pack in the United States.

The controversies provoked by the Penn-Marydel hound among hunting people are not new. In 1936, two years after the breed was formally established, John B. Hannum was mounting the same defense we hear today. In answer to the question "What qualities should you seek in a hound," he wrote:

> I know that the average, indeed the great average, will tell you that he must have good feet, well-sprung ribs, a certain kind of loin, hock, bone, etc. And so he should, but he doesn't hunt the fox with his feet, his loins, his legs or his ribs. He hunts it with his nose, his head, and his heart, and while these other attributes should not be disregarded, get the proper countenance first. The easiest thing in the world to breed is feet, ribs, bone etc., and the hardest, fox sense without cunning, good cry, good nose and gameness. (*Horse and Horseman*, September 1936)

That the Rose Tree should, after nearly one hundred fifty years, still be hunting this type of hound may be notable. More notable still, however, is that M. Roy Jackson's grandson, Jody Murtagh, is Master and huntsman of this venerable club today.

Murtagh's pedigree goes back to Masters and huntsmen on both sides. While M. Roy Jackson was his maternal grandfather, Jody's paternal grandfather, J. C. Murtagh, was MFH of the West Chester hounds early in the twentieth century. Jody's father, J. T. Murtagh, was MFH and huntsman of that pack for twenty years.

This prepotent Murtagh hunting line should continue for at least two generations into the future. Murtagh's daughters, Kerrie and Missy, serve as Field Master and whipper-in respectively. (Missy takes the horn when her father is unable to hunt.) And Kerrie's daughters—thirteen-year-old Codie and eight-year-old Katie Hayes—raise and train the Rose Tree puppies and show the hounds at the hound shows. Codie, five generations removed from M. Roy Jackson, handled the now famous Rose Tree Needy 2002 to the Grand Championship of the Virginia Foxhound Show last year.

THE ROSE TREE FOXHUNTING CLUB TODAY

The kennels and hunt stables of the Rose Tree Foxhunting Club were moved from the Philadelphia suburb of Media in 1961 and are today situated in Brogue, Pennsylvania, home of the current Master, Jody Murtagh, and his wife, Barbara. Brogue is a small farming community near York in the southern part of the state.

Both kennels and stables are housed in an ancient and charming two-story, vertical-sided barn that the Murtaghs restored and remodeled for hounds and horses. Separated by a gravel courtyard and grass circle, the barn sits no more than seventy-five feet from the Murtagh house, yet the setting remains quiet and serene. This reporter overnighted in a room facing the courtyard and never once heard the slightest murmur from a hound.

"When we moved here, that end of the barn looked like it had been hit with a Scud missile," said Murtagh. "It was caved in and nearly totally collapsed."

Working with a set of jacks, cranked up an inch or so every couple of days, it took nearly two years for the Murtaghs to raise the beams back into position, reset the supporting posts, and replace the siding and roof on the refurbished end.

"I'm sure that barn restoration helped our relations with the farmers here," Murtagh added. "They were probably afraid we would tear it down and replace it with a big aluminum building!"

Indeed, landowner relations at Rose Tree are excellent. The hunt kennels are situated in the northern portion of their hunting country, which covers roughly fifteen miles east to west and another fifteen miles north to south. The country consists of rolling crop fields—wheat, corn, and beans—separated by wooded coverts and moderately steep wooded ridges with stream beds—runs—in the bottoms, whose waters eventually reach the Susquehanna River—the eastern boundary of the country—some seven miles east of the kennels. The Susquehanna flows south from there another thirty miles before emptying into the northern end of Chesapeake Bay at Havre de Grace, Maryland.

HUNTING WITH THE PENN-MARYDELS

I was at ringside in May 2004 when Judge C. Martin Wood, MFH, stunned the crowd by naming Rose Tree Needy Grand Champion of the Virginia Foxhound Show, the first Penn-Marydel ever to be crowned grand champion of any MFHA-sanctioned hound show. So it was a treat to see Needy in the pack of fifteen-and-a-half couple that Murtagh took out this day.

Most huntsmen, I'm certain, hate to have someone riding in their back pocket when they are hunting hounds, but Murtagh graciously gave me the chance, and I took it. This was my first experience hunting closely enough with a pack of Penn-Marydels to watch them work, and I truly loved what I saw.

They worked quietly and diligently in covert, encouraged by Murtagh's voice, which he used periodically to encourage them and keep them focused on the job at hand. When a hound did speak, others stopped and listened for his or her affirmation. When a hound became sufficiently enthusiastic, they honored him right away by flying to him. Most of the times that they converged, they immediately agreed, gave a mighty roar, and began as a pack to actively sort out the direction taken by their quarry, helping one another and trying to settle to the line.

During the course of the day, four good foxes were found. Some of the coverts were large, and I have seen English and Crossbred hounds, with all the *drive* ascribed to those types, struggle to push their foxes out of the protection of large coverts. However, I can tell you that the Rose Tree hounds pushed their foxes out into the open with dispatch. With their voices ringing through the woods and their accuracy following the scent, foxes were viewed time and again bursting out of covert and taking the straightest and fastest line across wide open country toward their next refuge.

CHARLES JAMES, OPPORTUNIST

One reads and hears of foxes running through cattle or sheep to confuse hounds with other odors and distractions. I saw a new trick this day.

Hounds had found their second fox and were hunting it well through a large covert bisected by a line of immense power-line towers. Murtagh, who leaves his hounds alone when they are hunting well, positioned us at one end where we could look down the wide swath cleared for the towers.

The clamor of hounds increased, becoming louder and more thrilling as they worked steadily toward us. The fox would have to appear soon if he valued his brush. We watched, waited, and there he stole, from the tip of the woods nearest us into the gap of the power line.

Without hesitating, the fox made a right-hand turn and headed straight for a group of turkey vultures feasting on the remains of a dead raccoon. He ran directly for the carcass, putting the vultures to flight, and continued on into the woods on the other side of the gap.

A clever ruse, but it didn't work. Hounds raced out of the covert singing to the line, the front-runners flashing over the fox's turn only momentarily. Their heads came up, they whirled about, and, with the help of those behind, recovered the line in a matter of seconds. All business, they ran on, ignoring the dead raccoon, disappearing once again into the other half of the covert, and very soon pushing their fox into the open on the other side.

It was galloping gear again for huntsman and his shadow, with hounds ahead in the open, packed together, swinging with their line, singing their enthusiasm, their supreme delight in fulfilling their reason to be. Hounds finally put their fox to ground on the wooded hillside of a ravine we had climbed up and scrambled down several times in pursuit.

Hounds found and hunted four foxes during the course of the day, all of which ran well and far. Hounds found the line of the last fox as Murtagh was roading the pack to his next draw. They came to-gether in a crash of music and were off once again across the fields and into a large impenetrable cover. Missy galloped off to the east, Murtagh to the west with me in his wake. This time Murtagh and I were thrown out completely, and, after galloping fruitlessly in search, we pulled up on the crest of a hill to listen. Not a sound. I couldn't resist saying, "Tell the truth, Jody. Don't you wish you were carrying a radio with you right now?"

Murtagh smiled. "Well, I do have a cell phone in my pocket if it comes to that!" he said.

Going on, we found Barbara on the road with all the hounds in the truck. Missy had got with hounds, stayed with them until they marked the fox to ground, then collected them and loaded them into the truck!

We had a long hack home, but it was the slow, satisfied, contented sort of hack that comes after a good day's sport—the body pleasantly weary, the horse moving rhythmically and softly, the breeze kind.

Some Penn-Marydel packs are said to hunt the line slowly and meticulously, speaking enthusiastically, as the field follows at a walk. Perhaps in such instances they are giving a level of sport under conditions that would completely stymie other hounds. Or perhaps this is a function of their breeding, culling, or how they are handled in the field by their huntsman. I cannot say. What I can say, however, is that anyone who doubts the ability of Penn-Marydels to run should hunt with the Rose Tree pack. Then decide.

20

A BOLD EXPERIMENT AT MR. STEWART'S CHESHIRE FOXHOUNDS

2005

The drastic change in Cheshire's breeding program described in this story was wrenching for many members of this venerable hunt. Emotions notwithstanding, there is little disagreement that the newly developed hound pack delivers excellent hunting for a discerning and hard-riding membership.

By crossing Penn-Marydels with English hounds, the Cheshire Masters and huntsman are striving to produce a Crossbred hound that combines the voice and low scenting attributes of the Penn-Marydel with the drive of the English foxhound. With five years having passed since the story was written, I asked MFH Russell Jones for an update.

"We are developing a new type of hound, and it's a long-term process," Jones said. "Since we are only hunting bitches, we have forced ourselves to go outside for semen. We are maintaining both our purebred lines—Penn-Marydel and English—for future brood bitches. The real question becomes who to breed the Crossbred daughters to."

As examples, Jones explained that a Crossbred bitch needing more voice might be bred to a Penn-Marydel dog, or a Crossbred bitch that tended to be shy might be bred to an English dog.

"Our challenge is to correctly identify the aptitudes of the Crossbred daughters so we can breed them right," Jones said.

One might well wonder how three disparate hound types work together in the pack.

"They hunt great together," said Jones, "and they respect each other." Jones and his hunt staff are convinced that the hounds of each breed value the attributes brought to the pack by the other.

It was a special treat to see the beautiful hunting country of Mr. Stewart's Cheshire Foxhounds. Here, a scant twenty-five miles from the outskirts of the city of Philadelphia, a foxhunter's paradise has been preserved by the herculean efforts and unrelenting will of Mrs. John B. Hannum, MFH of the Cheshire for fifty-eight years. Throughout her years as Master, she saw to it that properties coming onto the market were purchased by hunt members, placed in conservation easement, then resold. In 1967, George "Frolic" Weymouth and other members of the hunt formed the renowned Brandywine Conservancy, which has to date permanently protected more than thirty-eight thousand acres of land in the area.

On Sunday, after the conclusion of the MFHA board meeting, visiting Masters were invited to visit the Cheshire kennels—a lovely old brick structure built in the 1930s and still serving the foxhounds well. Professional huntsman Ivan Dowling, with the help of professional whipper-in Sam Clifton, showed the Cheshire hounds and explained their breeding program.

The pack underwent a major change just a couple of years ago, when Dowling's predecessor, John Tullock, became huntsman. Tullock drafted most of the Old English hounds and introduced Penn-Marydels—mostly Rose Tree breeding—to the pack. Dowling, who whipped-in to Tullock, has continued the program since Tullock's departure.

It was a fascinating kennel visit in light of the fact that Dowling, under the supervision of MFH Russell Jones, has gone to an all-bitch pack and is breeding a new type of Crossbred foxhound, using primarily American Penn-Marydel and modern English bloodlines, along with some Old English lines. That amounts to three ingredients, but it's really more complicated in that some of their modern English types are really crosses on Fell, Welsh, English, Walker, and Midland.

"We are trying to breed an *elite* foxhound," explained Jones. "We don't yet know what the pedigree mix of that will be. This is a long-term proposition. We're trying to create a hound with hybrid vigor that we can breed from. If we can keep enough voice and nose in our crosses, we may breed back to the English. Right now we are crossing in both directions—Penn-Marydel and English—and we'll see what we get."

"The hounds were healthy and pleasing to look at," said Association President Mason Lampton, MFH. "I'm thrilled that Masters and staff are excited and have a direction to pursue. They want cry, and they're going to a source of cry [the Penn-Marydels]. They're building a pack to hunt the red fox and to meet the needs of their country," Lampton added.

Former president Daphne Wood, MFH, who loves the modern English foxhound, hopes that Cheshire will keep a substantial percentage of English bloodlines in their Crossbreds. "I was very impressed with Ivan and Sam," she said. "It's nice to see promising young professionals coming along. They handled the hounds very well, I thought. And the Penn-Marydels will add deeper cry and some sport on a poor scenting day."

The visitors who stayed to hunt with the Cheshire on Monday were well rewarded. This is a unique hunting experience. We've all heard that some foxhunters hunt to ride and some ride to hunt. It seems, however, that the Cheshire field hunts to jump! No queuing up at panels for this field; the country is fenced with split-rail line fencing, well set back from the roads, and all riders point their horses at their own set of rails. Of course, it stands to reason that a good horse is needed when you are among a field of jump race riders, open jumper competitors, Maryland Hunt Cup winners, and following

The Cheshire foxhound pack is made up of pure Penn-Marydels, pure English foxhounds, and Crossbreds of those two breeds.   *Noel Mullins photo*

Cheshire huntsman Ivan Dowling (shown) and staff are mounted on ex-racehorses, either off the flat track or the steeplechase course. Dowling and staff need to move along ahead of a hard riding field.   *Noel Mullins photo*

Field Master Bruce Miller, himself an ex-race rider and current steeplechase trainer.

I knew my horse Smasher had the scope for any size fence, yet I knew he could be a cheat on occasion. So, at dinner the evening before, I enlisted Beth LaMotte,* the sister of my old Massachusetts friend Russell Clark, to baby-sit me the next day.

True to her word, bless her, Beth and her husband, Clipper, met me at the meet and took me under their wing. On the way to the first covert, a solid fence presented itself in the distance.

"Stay with Beth," said Clipper, "I have to go to the back for a moment."

---

*If you remember the all-time favorite (July 2006) *Covertside* cover featuring "The Muddy Lady," then you've seen the unsinkable Beth LaMotte.

It was the old ruse. It had been played on me before, yet it's a darned good idea. The poor LaMottes, having been saddled with the responsibility of keeping me healthy, needed to know whether they could hunt up front in their usual position or whether they had best discreetly move to the back with me.

Fortunately, Smasher was thinking forward, we met the fence well, and flew over. Within seconds Clipper galloped alongside and, smiling broadly, exclaimed that I had handled the fence better than most of the field. I had passed the first test!

Hounds found, and we raced over the beautiful Cheshire country flying the rail fences with the best of them. I'm afraid I was concentrating more on the imposing fences than on the hound work, but it was totally exhilarating, and I began to relax on my horse. Big mistake.

After jumping all the post-and-rail fences, we came to a fallen log in the woods across the trail at which my horse stopped dead at the very last stride. I flew off, managed to hang onto the reins, jumped up, and pulled him off the trail so the rest of the field could pass. Beth and Clipper cheerfully stayed with me until I remounted. Someone once told me that if I couldn't take being humbled every so often, I shouldn't ride horses. How true.

On the last run of the day, I had an opportunity to redeem myself somewhat. Galloping up front once again, with hounds running on ahead, a single section of a rail fence positioned in a gap between a hedgerow presented itself. I noticed some riders pulling out and taking a different tack. My pilots, Beth and Clipper, however, rode straight at it and went on. It was easily over four feet high . . . and airy. Mindful of my earlier embarrassment, I laid both legs on Smasher. He flew it perfectly, and I still remember how long it took to come down to earth again before galloping on.

The Cheshire pack finished an excellent day of sport with this spectacular run at the end which, after four hours in the saddle, left the field with an hour's hack back to the meet.

Tony Leahy, MFH, hunted up with huntsman Dowling, and he was impressed with the Cheshire staff.

"The hounds were hunted in a lovely way," Leahy said. "Ivan has a cool head and a nice quiet way of hunting hounds. He was honest with them as opposed to putting on a show for the visitors." Speaking of the breeding program, Leahy added, "They're attempting to move forward. I definitely plan to come back to see how the program progresses."

"The pack harked to each other beautifully, ran well, and showed great sport," said Mason Lampton. "They had tremendous cry and were very responsive to the staff."

"They certainly had great cry," agreed Daphne Wood, "but I noticed some high-mouthed white hounds [read English!] driving the fox hard on the front end of the pack!"

So the friendly controversy goes on—English versus American—and long may it last!

21

LION HOUNDS IN THE JUAN TOMAS PACK

2005

Lion hounds sometimes pursue their quarry for days. They can't switch lions, they can't give up, and they need good voices so their huntsman can find them. This is how the huntsman makes his living, and he can't afford to feed fools. Are these traits useful in a foxhound pack? Jim Nance, MFH of the Juan Tomas Hounds in New Mexico, where lion hunting goes back to the nineteenth century, thinks so.

Where might you go to add voice and drive to your pack? It might not occur to those of us east of the Mississippi, but some MFHA-Recognized hunts routinely bring lion hounds into their packs for just those qualities. In fact, the MFHA accepts cat or lion hounds into the *Foxhound Kennel Studbook* if the breeder attests that three generations of the hound in question have hunted cat.

In the nineteenth century, lion and bear hunting in the West was carried on by hound men hired by ranchers to curb predation of their livestock. Many of these old-timers earned legendary reputations and sometimes acted as hunting guides to sportsmen from the East and from Europe. Teddy Roosevelt, for one, loved to travel west for the excitement of arduous hound hunts on foot, horseback, or mule that lasted sometimes for days at a time on the track of a single quarry.

Lion and bear populations are still high in many Western ranching countries, and, not surprisingly, this same style of hunting endures to this day for the very same reasons—predation control and sport. And drafts from today's lion hunters into MFHA-Recognized packs carry bloodlines that trace back to those early times and the legendary lion and bear hunters like Ben Lilly, Montague Stevens, and the Evans brothers.

The mountain lion (also known as cougar or puma) still thrives in New Mexico. Jim Nance, MFH of the Juan Tomas Hounds, has been a racehorse and cattle breeder all his life, and he has applied that experience to the breeding of his hounds. His Joint-Master, Mrs. Helen Kruger, is one of the MFHA's longest-serving Masters. It was she who saw a beautiful mountain lion hound bitch and suggested they introduce lion hounds into the pack to help them hunt coyote.

"There are thirteen subspecies of coyotes in the United States," explained Nance. "We hunt three of those. One is called *lestes*, which is a mountain coyote; another subspecies we hunt is *latrans*, a plains coyote; and the third subspecies is called *mearns*, a desert coyote. On our ranch, which is more than six thousand feet above sea level, we have a lot of flat area. That's where these desert coyote are. On the sides of the flat area, the mesa rises two or three thousand feet higher. That's where we get these mountain coyote. Then some of our hunting country intersects with the plains on the east side of the Rocky Mountains, and we get the plains coyote.

"The mountain coyotes, *lestes*, are really dark, and they're bigger. The plains coyotes, *latrans*, are pretty good size, too. The desert coyote, *mearns*, is smaller, lanky, and fast—they're all fast!—but *mearns* is really fast and the hardest to hunt. Living out in the open, they *have* to work harder."

Nance's hunting country is dry, with only eight to fourteen inches of rain a year. But he figures if they can hunt lions and bears in these conditions, he should be able to hunt coyote. Whether cat hounds have lower scenting abilities than traditional foxhounds, Nance won't

Ben Lilly hunted mountain lion and bear for ranchers throughout the Southwest more than a hundred years ago. The bloodlines of his hounds are in some of our foxhound packs today.

say. What he does maintain is that cat hounds, having been hunted in his country for more than a hundred years, may be more adapted to the conditions through selective breeding.

In appearance, cat hounds are no different from foxhounds. The lines in Nance's kennels were originally blue Gascons that came from France.

"Ben Lilly, who hunted bear and cat here more than a hundred years ago, came from Louisiana. That would explain how he came to bring French hounds. But, if you were to spray-paint one, you would have a hard time distinguishing it from a Virginia Bywaters–type foxhound," says Nance.

Nance breeds for size even though some huntsmen maintain that smaller hounds get through the brush more easily. "It's like the difference between a small horse and a big horse," says Nance. "A small horse can run really fast, but the horse with the longer legs will be faster in the long run. I go for a deep chest, like a Thoroughbred horse. Muscular. A big, strong dog that can race."

Nance maintains an image of his ideal hound in his mind's eye, and when he sees it he goes to the breeder. He has five basic types in his pack—a lot of Larry Pitts' Potomac Hunt (MD) hounds that go back to the Bywaters hound. Nance loves their biddability, their looks, and their hunting ability.

He also maintains lines in his kennels from two hounds that he bought even before becoming involved in the breeding of this pack. One was a strain of Goodman called a Goodman Walker from Oklahoma. This hound had a good nose and size. Another was a pure Walker he got from a night hunter. The hound's brother was a Missouri State Champion night hunter. Nance appreciates the drive in the Walker hounds even though they are less biddable.

His lion hounds are Ben Lilly, Evans brothers, and Orville Fletcher lines.

"These men were all famous lion hunters," Nance says. "The hounds have nose, biddability, drive, and really deep voices. Lion hounds often trail their quarry for ten to twelve hours, and they can't switch. I know of one hunt where Orville Fletcher followed one lion halfway across New Mexico."

Lastly, he still has a small percentage of English bloodlines in the pack that came from the Arapahoe Hunt (CO). Mrs. Kruger brought those drafts in years ago, and they're still important to the breeding program.

Nance recognizes that all these strains have their individual traits, but feels they also have a lot of qualities in common. He has given some hounds with his foxhound bloodlines back to lion hunters and is pleased that these man like them for lion hunting. Orville Fletcher, one of the old-timers still actively hunting, named one of them Sleuth—from a story by Montague Stevens—which Nance takes as a huge compliment.

Lion hunting today is both a necessity and a sport. Some of the lions' favorite food is baby horses and baby calves, and they devastate

For additional reading on lion and bear hunting in the old South-west, try:

- *Meet Mr. Grizzly,* by Montague Stevens
- *Ben Lilly's Tales of Bears, Lions and Hounds,* edited by Neil B. Carmony
- *Hunting Grizzlys, Black Bear and Lions "Big-Time" on the Old Ranches,* by Will Evans
- *Slash Ranch Hounds,* by G. W. "Dub" Evans

Find these and other out-of-print books at www.abebooks.com.

the deer. Although the lion hunting season coincides with winter in New Mexico (like foxhunting), it's legal on private land there through-out the year. One large landowner who introduced Rocky Mountain Big Horn Sheep into the country had to do a lot of culling of lions on his ranch because they really loved to eat his sheep.

As a sport, lion hunting is big business. In Nance's part of New Mexico, good professional guides charge five to ten thousand dollars to take a hunter lion hunting. Hunters come from Europe and else-where, and there's no shortage of mountain lions.

Some guides go out on horses, some on mules, and sometimes on foot. Traditionally, the huntsman follows his hounds until a track is found, then he follows the hounds until they find the lion.

"A lion run is just like foxhunting, except it's rougher," says Nance. "One of the main qualities of the lion hounds is they are the most biddable hounds I've ever seen. Lion hunters hunt alone, or at most with one or two other people. There are no whippers-in and no outriders, and it all takes place in rough, vast country. A lion hound has to do what you want for hours, sometimes days on end, out of love and respect."

22

THE COAL VALLEY HOUNDS

Speedways and Roller Coasters

2005

In order to interpret and report accurately in Covertside *on the aims and actions of the Masters of Foxhounds Association, I regularly attended the three directors meetings held each year. Traditionally, the New York directors meeting is followed in the evening by the annual Masters Dinner. Since I was listed as an honorary member of the association, I was graciously invited to join the directors and visiting Masters from around the country at that very colorful dinner.*

After dinner it was the practice for many of the Masters—men still in their white ties and scarlet tails, women in elegant evening dresses—to repair to one of the hotel lounges for a nightcap. One such evening at the Oak Bar in the Plaza, I found myself sitting next to a most attractive couple. The lady smote me with a dazzling smile.

"I'm Kathleen Sandness, and this is my husband, Wes," she said. "We're Joint-Masters of a new hunt, the Coal Valley Hounds in Kansas."

"You're going to Kansas? For foxhunting?" This from my friend as we hacked contentedly—and a long hack it was—back to the meet after a very good day's sport across the Virginia countryside.

"Hey," I replied, defensively, "there's a lot of good hunting that goes on in unlikely places."

Come to think of it, though, Kansas isn't so very unlikely. The Fort Leavenworth Hunt was registered by the MFHA in 1929, and famous American military figures—Generals Jonathan Wainwright, Gordon Sullivan, and William Hoge—honed their riding skills following hounds there. The Mission Valley Hunt was registered even earlier—1927—and its huntsman for the last quarter-century, Tommy Jackson, enjoys a stellar reputation in "elite" hunting circles. Which brings us to the third Kansas hunt: the Coal Valley Hounds, registered just three years ago.

Situated in southeastern Kansas, Coal Valley finds itself only about a two-hour drive from both Kansas hunts and about the same from the Misty River Hounds in Arkansas and the Harvard Fox Hounds in Oklahoma. I was to discover that the sportsmen and women of the area support all the hunts by traveling these distances routinely, many belonging to more than one.

Drs. Wes and Kathleen Sandness founded the Coal Valley Hounds on their Wesbrook Bar-X Ranch in McCune, Kansas. They have acquired additional land contiguous to the ranch, including the B and N Ranch, where the hunt stables and clubhouse are now located and

Coal Valley Masters with visitor (left to right): Dr. Anthony Adams, Dr. Kathleen Sandness, Tommy Jackson, Norm Fine, Stephen Satterlee, and Dr. Wes Sandness.   *Ray Orth photo*

which is now the center of Wes's cow-calf operation. The two ranches plus Wes's other holdings give hounds three to four thousand acres over which to pursue the coyote (and the occasional fox). Neighboring ranches add another ten thousand acres to the Coal Valley hunting country.

Wes and Kathleen are still members of the Mission Valley Hunt near Kansas City, where they started their hunting experience. Mission Valley huntsman Tommy Jackson was so impressed with their country that he gave them hounds and urged them to start their own hunt. Jackson, in addition to his duties at Mission Valley, now shares Joint-Master status at Coal Valley with Wes and Kathleen; Dr. Anthony Adams, a physician; and Stephen Satterlee, a retired businessman.

DETOUR

Except for one wild and improbable detour, Wes Sandness's track from boyhood to eventually becoming Master and huntsman of his own pack was a reasonably straight line. As a boy in Illinois, Wes had beagles, then a few foxhounds. He and his pals hunted rabbit on foot with shotguns and sat among the ravines listening to the foxhounds push the fox. He was riding broncs at the age of twelve. But after finishing high school, Wes veered adventurously from the country life, left home, and headed for the bright lights and a singing career!

"I had several radio shows. Then one day I was performing at the county fair in Greenville, Illinois, and a representative from the *Ted Mack Amateur Hour* came up to me. He invited me to New York for an audition, and I wound up on national TV."

Once in New York, Wes appeared in musicals—playing many roles, including Sky Masterson in *Guys and Dolls*—but his great love was oratorio and concert opera.

"There is no scarier or more wonderful feeling than standing on a stage with the orchestra in front and the choir behind you, filling the hall with music. There's nothing like it," Wes recalled. "But that was a long time ago, another chapter in my life."

One day he walked off the set at NBC, thought hard about his future, went home, and entered college. He earned a PhD from Indiana University and began a long and satisfying career, eventually becoming Dean of the College of Education and Vice President of Student Affairs at the University of Pittsburg in Kansas. The president of the university, George Budd, was his mentor, father figure, and friend. The pair traveled the horse show circuit showing Morgans. Wes was also an R-rated AHSA judge. And that's how Wes met Kathleen.

Kathleen grew up in San Antonio, Texas (which accounts for the chili peppers served with eggs every morning for breakfast). A natural athlete—collegiate swimmer (ranked sixth in the nation) and horsewoman—she met Wes while training and showing Morgans on the Southwestern circuit. She gave that up after marrying Wes in 1978, returned to school, and studied medicine.

With Kathleen immersed in a demanding curriculum, Wes found himself with time on his hands. He discovered the Mission Valley Hunt and was soon filling his spare time with a new activity: mounted foxhunting. Today, Kathleen practices internal medicine in Pittsburg, Kansas; Wes, retired from his academic career, is a full-time rancher; and the Coal Valley Hounds is their joint adventure. And Wes's old mentor and friend, George Budd—now ninety years old but still tall, straight, and handsome—mounted a horse for Opening Meet this year and regularly follows by vehicle on the road.

PLUNDER AND RECLAMATION

The Coal Valley Hounds take their name from the region's major commercial activity that was carried on in southeastern Kansas for most of the twentieth century: coal mining—both strip mining and deep shaft mining. Coal towns sprang to life throughout the early 1900s. Nearby Stone City, once boasting a population of twelve thousand, is now, like many others, a ghost town, with remnants of the brick bank vault the only visible evidence remaining. The entire area was undermined by deep shafts, and the surface was stripped by enormous machines that gouged the countryside following the veins of coal.

Slag and shale were dumped alongside the trench as the machines proceeded, forming a high ridge parallel to each trench. When the end of the vein was reached, the machines turned around and repeated the process on a parallel course—digging and piling. What remained after the coal was removed were thousands of acres denuded and trenched in wavy corrugations.

When, in the 1970s, the federal government stepped in with regulations intended to reduce the occupational hazards and reclaim the ruined countryside, the mining companies gradually lost their profit incentives. Slowly, the industry declined, then died. Mining companies filed for bankruptcy, and land changed hands for ten dollars an acre. Thanks to the law of unintended consequences, however, this story has a happy ending.

The slow process of reclaiming the land began. Trenches were back-filled, but because the material pushed back couldn't make up for the volume of coal that was extracted, the terrain remained corrugated, though a bit softer. The last pits dug were left unfilled and are now waterways—deep water—thirty to forty feet deep in some places—good trout habitat. And bass.

Native grasses returned. Trees and cover grew in the valleys and on the ridges, providing habitat for abundant wildlife. What was once an eyesore is now an asset. Today the area is a sportsman's paradise with ranch land selling for fifteen hundred dollars an acre. Deer, wild turkey, bobcat, rabbit, upland game birds, ducks—all species of wildlife abound—including the ubiquitous coyote.

THE DUMPS: EYESORE TO ASSET

The Coal Valley hunting country is bisected by roads—many still gravel—laid out in a rectilinear grid of one-mile by one-mile "sections." Within these sections there are areas of flat, open pasture as well as areas known locally as "the dumps": the corrugated remains of seventy-five years of corporate insensitivity. The Coal Valley hounds hunt through all this country, streaking across the flat lands and plunging through the dumps.

As is the case with most new packs, the Coal Valley hounds are an eclectic mix of drafts from around the country. Assembled just four years ago, hounds have been obtained from Bijou Springs (CO), Arapahoe (CO), Wabash (NE), Gamble Hill (IA), Fort Leavenworth (KS), Mission Valley (KS), Misty River (AR), Warrenton (VA), Hillsboro (TN), and Long Run (KY). There are American and Crossbred drafts, English from the Arapahoe, Hardaway bloodlines from Misty River, and even four Penn-Marydels (not yet entered) from Long Run.

Wes hunts the hounds, and his main thrust has been toward a Crossbred pack. One stallion line in particular that he likes is that of Coal Valley Jackson 2002 (Warrenton Kilroy 1998 - Fort Leavenworth Foxy 1999), a former stallion hound class winner at the Central States Hound Show. Tommy Jackson drafted his namesake, full of Mission Valley blood, to Coal Valley, and Wes put Jackson to Gamble Hills Roulette 1994 (North Hills Gimlet 1990 - Tryon Raisin 1989). Jackson, a Crossbred dog hound, goes back in tail male to the Fernie (UK); Roulette, an American bitch, goes back tail female to Piedmont (VA) breeding.

"Roulette had an excellent nose, and her litter by Jackson is now in the pack. One of them, a little second-year bitch named Blossom, was right in at the kill on Opening Meet and also put a coyote to ground in a culvert that day. Our hounds are different looking, but they hunt as a pack," Wes added. "They're biddable, yet eager."

That was very much the case during my two days in the field with them. Wes hunts them quietly and patiently, and all the hounds pitch in and do the hard work. Scenting was particularly difficult on the first day, yet they worked the coverts diligently. They found, trailed, lost, and worked to regain the line again and again. Despite the dry conditions—dust was flying—and twenty-knot winds from the south, hounds managed to give the field a good four-mile chase before the Master blew for home.

Conditions improved the second day. All told, five coyotes were viewed, and the field enjoyed two blistering runs. My eye, tuned to the red foxes in my home hunting country, struggled to pick up the coyotes even after hearing the *view holloas*. My best view came as we crossed the big pastures of the B and N Ranch. Riding with Wes, I heard the *tally-hos* behind me. Straining my eyes to see what everyone else seemed to have no trouble seeing, I finally managed to pick up the lone coyote perhaps three-quarters of a mile away, loping gently away left-handed. Hounds were already screaming on the line a good quarter of a mile ahead by the time I saw our quarry. Wes dug his heels into his horse and flew, me in his wake, after hounds. Hounds gained another quarter of a mile on us as we circumnavigated a long fence line.

Wes likes his whippers-in either out on the gravel roads or able to get there quickly in case he needs them to get ahead and view the coyote across, turn the coyote, or stop the pack for any reason. He, like most huntsmen chasing the fleet coyote, makes good use of his radio to communicate with both his mounted whippers-in and his wheel-whip in the truck.

As we hammered across the grazing land I watched the course of the coyote, a small dot moving steadily away in the distance. We finally gained the road—Sixtieth—and galloped on down the gravel surface.

Wes got on the radio again at a dead run. "Kathleen, go down Liberty and around to Fiftieth [one mile between Sixtieth and Fiftieth]. If he crosses, stop the hounds."

Fortunately, the coyote crossed Sixtieth and stayed in the country. We jumped into the next section over a tiger trap made of hefty logs with a good drop on the landing side. They call this fence the "Death Trap," I later learned. Superbly mounted on an experienced Thoroughbred called Mike, however, it was all the same to me. At a brief check I turned and saw MFH Satterlee grinning broadly at me.

"Isn't this great?" he demanded with enthusiasm.

Satterlee has come to foxhunting through the involvement of his wife, Susan, and obviously has caught the spirit. A thorough sportsman, he generally spends the early morning hours rough shooting before tacking up for a meeting of hounds.

Abruptly we were in a wooded landscape, plunging down into the pits, climbing the "over-burden" (narrow ridges of piled-up slag), plunging and climbing as on a roller coaster, following narrow trails worn through the brush, bushes, and trees. Tough country, especially for the huntsman trying to stay with hounds. Good cry is needed, and Wes's Coal Valley Crossbred hounds can really fill the dumps with music.

Hounds worked their way through the rough, pushed the quarry back into the open, and, as we ran him westerly, more *tally-hos* were heard. Two coyotes, and a split pack. By the time Wes and staff got their pack back together and on the line, the hunted coyote had a commanding lead. Continuing his westerly course, he finally ran out of the country. This hunt had taken us through six or seven sections, more than seven miles as hounds ran.

One of the advantages of meeting at the B and N Ranch is the proximity to the Coal Valley clubhouse—the old ranch house. It's right there by the hunt stables, and embraces all weary, thirsty, and hungry participants at the end of the day. Food preparation is a shared effort, and hunt breakfasts are satisfying, convivial, and also entertaining. Member Ray Orth, the hunt's mounted photographer, slips the storage device from his digital camera into his laptop computer, and projects a repeating slide show of the day's events for everyone's amusement.

So, yes, I went to Kansas for foxhunting—or more accurately coyote hunting—and found a group of sportsmen and women who hunt (as that great Tennessee story-teller Henry Hooker likes to say) "for the pure, 'blime fun of it!" In doing so, they are putting their own American stamp on the sport. They encourage and include everyone who wants to join in the fun, whether they first appear wearing tall hunt boots or cowboy boots. They support each other by traveling hours to meets of neighboring hunts. They throw after-hunt parties for the fun of socializing. At the same time, they respect and maintain the core traditions of attire and sportsmanship that lie at the foundation of this enduring sport. Here in the wide open spaces of this vast continent, North American foxhunting has a healthy future.

23

JUNIOR HUNTSMEN PRODUCE BIG SPORT AT BELLE MEADE

2006

There is no better effort a hunt can make for the future of hunting than to encourage juniors. Many hunts do it in a variety of ways: junior meets, hunting camps in the off season, and by reaching out to nearby Pony Clubs.

In Covertside *we urged Masters to invite competent juniors to the front every so often where they could watch hounds work. We suggested that juniors can even be useful up front, hopping off their ponies to open gates or holding the huntsman's horse if needed. We ran a cartoon series, "Mac and DeDe," primarily for juniors, that we hoped was both instructive and humorous. And we published foxhunting stories and poems by juniors that were often surprising in their perceptions, heartwarming in their innocence, and impressive in the talents displayed.*

Masters and hunt members often sent articles to Covertside *reporting on junior meets held by their hunt. Although I loved publishing articles on new ideas that other hunts could make use of, there wasn't much new about junior meets. And with only four issues a year, I often had to pass on the junior meet articles. Then one day Charlie Lewis came along with a different twist.*

"We're planning a joint junior meet with the Mells Fox Hounds," said Charlie Lewis, Joint-Master of the Belle Meade Hunt. "You ought to come and do a story."

Charlie could see I wasn't biting.

"We're doing it a little differently," he continued. "The juniors will hunt the hounds and whip-in."

Now, that *is* different.

"I'll be there!" I said.

The plan was for Chase Wilson (seventeen) and Dusten Harris (eighteen) to carry the horns for a combined Belle Meade and Mells pack. Each had hunted hounds only once before this occasion, though they were no strangers to the process. Chase whips-in to his father, Epp Wilson, Master and huntsman of the Belle Meade Hunt (GA). Dusten whips-in to her mother, Joy McCormick, Master and huntsman of the Mells Fox Hounds (TN).

My first recollection of Chase goes back seven years. He was ten. I had just arrived at Foxboro, the Wilsons' farm, when a boy on a pinto pony, energetically waving one arm over his head and using his voice like a hunting horn, came galloping into view, followed by six foxhound puppies. The small huntsman and his miniature pack disappeared into the woods only to reappear in a few minutes, still in full cry—the boy, not the puppies.

"That's my son, Chase," Epp had explained. "He takes care of the hound puppies, exercises them every day, and teaches them to follow."

That small boy has grown considerably in the past seven years.

Dusten's background is similar. In fact, eight members spanning three generations of her family were in the field this day to follow her lead: grandmother Anita Underwood; mother Joy and Joy's sister, Lisa Cowley, who also whips-in at Mells; Joy's younger daughter, Caitlyn McCormick, and sons, Clint and Zach McCormick; and Lisa's son, Cole.

PHOTO OP

I helped Epp load about a dozen scarlet hunt coats into his truck as we left for the meet at six a.m.

Epp Wilson, MFH, hauls a carload of scarlet coats to the junior meets for the photo ops. "The kids enjoy it, and it gives them something to look forward to," he says. Front row (left to right): Sutton Metz, Caitlyn McCormick, Lizzy Reed, Meagan Owen, Clint McCormick. Second row (left to right): Zach McCormick, Kayleigh Wilcher, Taylor Pritchard, Natalie Gilmore, Dusten Harris. Third row: Cole Cowley, Chase Wilson, Nichole Smith, Johnna Henley, Kristin Preston.   *Bella Vita Fotografie photo, www.bellavitafotografie.com*

"The kids put these on for their pictures before the meet," he explained. "Some of the kids are so small, the tips of their fingers barely stick out of the sleeves, but they enjoy it. It gives them something to look forward to: wearing a scarlet coat!"

The photography session completed—which involved much squirming, giggling, and grinning for the lens—foxhunters young and old climbed into the saddle. The two packs—eleven couple from each hunt—were put into a holding yard for a few minutes to get acquainted with each other. Chase and Dusten walked among the hounds in the yard, talking, soothing, petting.

It was nearly seven a.m., late April, and the weather promised "warm." Shirtsleeves were pronounced the uniform of the day, and jackets were shed. Hard as it must have been for Epp and Joy—the two regular huntsmen for these packs—they stayed well away as hounds left the yard to follow their youthful huntsmen across the road to the first draw. Before hounds even had a chance to put their noses down, Charlie Lewis, scouting on ahead, viewed a coyote. Hounds were brought to the view, and a day of sport as good as any day this reporter has seen this season began with an explosion of sound and motion.

TAKING HIS CHANCES WITH THE TURKEYS

It was early morning—cool and damp from rains the day before. Scenting must have been excellent, for the entire pack went away as one, fully in agreement that they had their olfactory sights set on their single mortal enemy. The Belle Meade hunting country is a combination of large wooded areas and open fields. There are good trails cut through woods, but they become narrow and trappy when plunging down into the many gullies and creek beds that bisect the woods. The country is well paneled with chicken coops set into the wire fencing.

Perhaps because of the large wooded areas and plentiful population of coyotes, the quarry tends to run in large circles, more like a red fox than your typical straight-out-of-the-country coyote. The thickness of the woods seems to reduce the speed factor as well, again giving the sport more of the flavor of a fox chase than a coyote race. The two huntsmen stayed well in touch with hounds through the woods, Chase choosing his trails deliberately and leading the way down and across the gullies when necessary.

At the infrequent checks, the junior huntsmen stood patiently, consulting each other, allowing hounds to work out the line, waiting until the general direction of hounds was reestablished before moving on. Once they moved on, however, they did so smartly, giving the field long gallops through the woods and across the open. Riding up with the huntsmen, my partner-for-the-day Jennifer Preston and I were able to gallop down the wood trails with the thrilling cry of hounds right beside us, mile upon mile, following every turn of the coyote.

Hounds checked several times near a gas pipeline clear-cut in the woods. At one check, a view was reported, and Chase and Dusten, realizing it could have been a second coyote, had to decide whether to bring hounds on or let them hunt. Since the scenting conditions were so good, they waited, and hounds rewarded their patience once again by recovering the line and resuming the chase.

The coyote, having completed one large circle in about thirty minutes, must have decided that he wasn't gaining any advantage. He ran down a hedgerow at the edge of a field and was viewed crossing Stagecoach Road heading for an area where turkey hunters were known to be pursuing their own elusive game. Hounds checked in the field, and Chase and Dusten stopped hounds at that point, rather than allowing them to recover the line and push on toward the road— always a fearful prospect—a decision that Epp praised later as he reviewed the run.

"Chase and Dusten showed the wisdom and presence of mind to say, 'All right, let's not run him that last quarter mile to get the last inch of this run and then have a chance of some of them crossing the road. Let's go on to the other coyote.'"

THE LUCKIEST COYOTE

The pack proved responsive and biddable to their young huntsmen, as they paused to collect hounds. The few stragglers returned readily to both horns. As we trotted with hounds toward where the fresh coyote had been viewed, I couldn't help recalling how well the pack had hunted on its own.

"Chase," I said. "Even *I* could hunt this pack of hounds."

He looked at me appraisingly.

"Yes, but could you *train* them to do that?" he retorted.

Point made.

The sun was rising, but it was still cool, and, apparently, scenting conditions were still good. Hounds jumped right on the line of the fresh coyote, and we were off once again in a chorus of hounds, clatter of hooves, and the occasional rap of a horse hitting a coop behind me. I was riding a 16.3-hand Canadian draft–Thoroughbred cross mare named Mary Kate that Chase's mother Sharon Wilson had chosen for me, and every time I heard the rap of a fence behind me, I mentally thanked Sharon for putting me on this excellent field hunter.

Our new pilot ran a similar route as that of his predecessor, and Chase kept us well in touch with the pack. Hounds checked yet again at the same gas pipeline. Chase looked at Dusten with a grin and a shrug in front of the coop that led to the clear-cut.

"Well, shall we jump this coop again?"

The music was glorious, hounds well together, and the pressure on the coyote was intense. He ran three large circles—crossing Stagecoach Road twice—but remained in good hunt-able country. Finally, after a full hour of running, with few checks, the music continued, but the motion stopped. The coyote was at bay.

We followed Chase and Dusten into the woods until we were stopped by a new barbed-wire fence. This was as close as we could get on horseback. The pair jumped off their horses, spread the barbed wire for each other to slip through, then slid down into the gully. Midst the splashing of hounds baying at the open end of an old drainage pipe into which the hunted coyote had taken refuge, the two young huntsmen, mud-spattered but flushed with success, received the congratulations of their proud parents. Junior field members followed, scrambling down the muddy banks into the wet bottom to gaze into the pipe, while the staff considered their strategy.

"The farmer wants this coyote killed," said Epp.

The pipe was about fifteen feet long, one end partially buried in the mud, the other end, into which the coyote had run, open. The pipe had served as a culvert for an old creek crossing, long since washed away, leaving just the pipe lying there in the bottom. The coyote had gone in about five or six feet and turned so his business end faced the opening, which was just large enough for a single hound to enter. Each time a hound crawled in, he quickly backed out with a bloody nose.

Hounds were removed, but nothing would entice the coyote to abandon his refuge. A long flexible PVC pipe arrived from the kennels and was inserted into the partially buried end of the culvert. After a few minutes of prodding, a very wet and muddy coyote shot out of the pipe like a ball from a cannon, scrambled up the bank, and was gone. Hounds were *holloaed* to the line, and huntsmen, staff, and field members pulled themselves out of the gully and ran back to their horses. The chase resumed, but twenty minutes in the pipe had given this coyote a much needed rest and had allowed the temperature to rise to the point where scenting became difficult. We ran for another twenty minutes, but at each check, hounds had increasing difficulty recovering the line.

We had enjoyed nearly three hours of hard hunting, and the toll was taken on hounds and horses. I was hearing some sharper raps on the fences behind me, and Mary Kate, whose gear of choice was "gallop" at the beginning of the day, now preferred to trot. The two young huntsmen had every right to be proud of the fact that they had accounted for their quarry, and it was decided to give this coyote best. It was but a short hack back to the kennels, the trailers, and Boots Hall, where a wonderful hot breakfast awaited us.

"What was the best part of the day for you guys?" I asked the two huntsmen.

"*Almost* getting the coyote," said Dusten.

"Charlie Lewis viewing that first coyote in the field. It made our job a whole lot easier!" said Chase.

"Yeah," I said with mock sarcasm. "I wanted to see you *draw* a covert and find one."

"Well," replied Chase, "it was all about placement. We had somebody in the right place!"

How can you argue with logic like that?

"OK, was there any time you were worried?" I asked the pair.

"Yeah, I thought the hounds would go to Wrightsboro Road," said Chase.

Dusten's worries, however, apparently took place well before the hunt. In fact, she kept her mother up most of the previous night by talking in her sleep. As Joy said, "I kept hearing Dusten say, 'Mason, pack in. Pack in, Mason. MASON!' I'd tell her, 'Mason's not here; go back to sleep.'"

This night we can assume everyone slept well, including the coyote.

~ 24 ~

FOXHOUND
PERFORMANCE TRIALS

A Good Test of a Hound?

2006–2007

When Midland MFH Ben Hardaway staged the first performance trials for Hardaway-type foxhounds ten years earlier, the rules of competition were taken from the foxhound field trials as have been practiced by night hunters and field trialers for a hundred years or more. These sportsmen seek to identify the best performing single hound in what is truly a hound race.

Early in the development of foxhound performance trials for mounted packs, experienced judges from field trials were invited to judge and teach us how to score hounds. During the course of one such early trial, I ignored a hound that I saw consistently skirting the pack and silently hitting the line ahead. To my mind, it was a cheat. The experienced field trial judge, however, had scored this hound well and often.

"I don't care if a hound skirts," he said in answer to my objection. "He wants to get there first."

That was an early example for me of the difference between what we seek in a pack hound and what the field trialer seeks in a hound race. In interviews, top huntsmen have often told me that they don't want individual stars. They want hounds with good noses, good cry, and good conformation that will work in the pack as helpful team members.

Since those early trials—with contributions by the MFHA's Dennis Foster; experienced trial huntsmen Tony Leahy (Fox River Valley) and Charles Montgomery (Live Oak); and Masters Epp Wilson (Belle Meade) and Max Naegler (Harvard Foxhounds)—I do believe that the format and rule changes have come a long way in identifying top-performing pack hounds deserving of the attention of Masters seeking good bloodlines to add to their own packs.

It was an honor for me to have been included in the roster of judges for the early trials. With the last Centennial trial, however, it was time to hang up my digital voice recorder and yellow armband. I didn't so much mind giving up the recorder, but that wonderful yellow armband! That was my passport to go anywhere and in any direction I wanted to score hounds. It was hard to give that up and return to my usual place in the field.

PREPARING FOR THE CENTENNIAL

Six Foxhound Performance Trials were held across the country during the 2005/2006 season in preparation for the Centennial Trials coming up the following season—testimony to the rising interest in these exciting events. Organizers fine-tuned their corps of volunteers, computer-savvy foxhunter Chris Towt revamped the laborious and time-consuming scoring system, and Masters carefully selected teams of hounds that would hopefully bring honor to their kennels by earning the title Centennial Hound.

Preparation trials were hosted by Misty River Hounds (AR), Belle Meade Hunt (GA), Aiken Hounds and Flat Branch Foxhounds (SC), Arapahoe Hunt (CO), West Hills Hunt (CA), and Sedgefield Hunt (NC). Thirty-one hunts entered hounds in the six trials, and the enthusiasm for this relatively new competition between hounds and their breeders hit an all-time high.

The winning foxhound in each trial is the one that compiles the highest total of combined points, calculated by a complex formula that uses data gathered by the judges over two days of hunting. Judges score hounds in four categories: *hunting, trailing, full cry,* and *marking*. The calculating formula factors in the relative importance of each of these categories for pack hunting and, by knowing the time that each score is recorded, rejects duplicate scores and factors in *endurance* as well.

I watch hounds work under the spectacular sheer rock wall bordering War Eagle Creek. *Akhtar Hussein photo*

Is the foxhound performance trial a good test of a foxhound? Every time I have sat as a judge in the scoring meetings held immediately after the hunts, I have been struck by the consistency of the judges' scoring. A handful of hounds will consistently attract scores from every judge. Other hounds are scored sporadically. Some hounds are hardly scored at all by any of the judges. Obviously, judges will not see every good deed accomplished by every hound, but the consistency of the scores attracted by the top performing hounds from all the judges convinces me that every hound that finishes in the top ten is an outstanding hound indeed.

Conditions—scenting or even terrain—are important factors that may favor one hound (or one hound type) over another on a particular day. Then conditions can change, and a hound that went unnoticed the previous day may be scored consistently by all the judges for outstanding work the second day. This implies that any judging of hounds is truly valid for just that day, under the conditions of that day, and in the particular country hunted. These caveats notwithstanding, many breeders are convinced that it makes more sense to breed to a proven performer than to a hound show champion. For this reason alone, performance trials may soon prove to make an important contribution to the foxhound in North America.

Judging Can Be Hazardous to Your Health

Being a judge at a foxhound performance trial can be the greatest of foxhunting fun. To score hounds, the judge must be close enough to see which hounds are doing the work and to read the numbers painted on their sides. This means getting very close to the action— as close as you can without interfering—closer sometimes than even the huntsman! Then, when hounds are running, the judge must try to get ahead of the pack in order to score the front-runners. (If you don't get the lead hound's number, you can't score any of the others behind him!)

Concentrating this way on one's mission inevitably leads to accidents, and the judges this year collected their share of breaks and bruises. Mitch Jacobs's horse carried him through a wire fence at the Central States Trial, then proceeded to walk on him, resulting in fractured facial bones. Mitch was a gamer, though. A handsome guy under normal conditions, he arrived at dinner that night, direct from the hospital, looking like he had been made up for a scene in a horror movie: flaming red eyeballs surrounded by black, blue, and violet flesh riddled with black stitching.

Dennis Foster's horse jumped *into* the ditch instead of over it at the Rocky Mountain trial in Colorado, resulting in a broken shoulder. (Dennis's, not the horse's.) As a result, Foster was unable to judge the season's final trial in North Carolina, the first trial he has missed since these competitions started.

Speaking of North Carolina, the trial organizers there warned the judges of two hazards in their country—bogs and stump holes. They even took the trouble to drive the judges through the country and show us what their bogs and stump holes looked like. Nevertheless, while attempting to catch up with the glorious cry of hounds reaching me through the trees, I managed to guide my horse directly into a stump hole. The horse went on his nose and I, after an initial touch-down, went airborne for what seemed like a long stunt flight before gravity reasserted itself. As I scrambled to my feet all I could think of was, 'I have no idea where I am, there's no one in sight, and if my horse runs off I'm sunk!' He—my wonderful horse, Guitar—trotted a large circle with the reins wrapped around his front foot, stopped, looked at me, and waited. Bless him.

Coping with Conditions

Changing conditions such as scent and terrain are to be expected, but foxhounds encountered some unexpected conditions as well. Hunting in the Ozarks of Arkansas at the Central States trial hosted by Dina Del Guercio's Misty River Hounds, visiting Masters were startled to learn that Dina, the trial huntsman, uses a cow horn rather than a copper horn. The visiting hounds hadn't a clue about responding to a cow horn. What to do? It was decided that Eleanor Hartwell, huntsman for the Bridlespur Hunt (MO), would accompany Dina and blow her copper horn when necessary.

Living in Virginia, where I can drive to ten hunts inside of an hour, it is heartwarming to see the enthusiasm with which members of the far-flung western hunts support their neighboring hunts. The four competing hunts at Misty River came to Arkansas from Iowa, Kansas, Missouri, and Oklahoma. Then after the hunt, when the scarlet coats, white breeches, and tall boots come off, the westerners revert to their core culture: jeans, cowboy boots, and western hats.

The highlight of hunting in the Misty River Hounds country came the second day. Master and huntsman Dina Del Guercio drew War Eagle Creek, where crystal-clear water runs over a firm bed of stones. On one side of the creek, a sheer rock wall face soars nearly a hundred feet in one breathtaking vertical leap. The rock face is punctuated here and there by small cavelike openings where red foxes make their dens.

On the other side of the creek is a gently undulating landscape of pasture, small meadows, and woodlands.

Hunting an All-Star Pack in Georgia

Michael Brown, huntsman for the Rappahannock Hunt in Virginia, served as trial huntsman at the Belle Meade trial. Each morning hounds met at 8:00 a.m. and by 8:05 they were in full cry. I asked Michael how the huntsman manages a high-mettled pack of hounds—the best from several hunts—that don't know each other and don't know the country.

"Hounds were mixed for a short time in the kennel yard before leaving the meet," Brown said. "That helps to get them acquainted. But my worst fear was that they would strike and start running immediately, which of course is exactly what happened! I was hoping they would have fifteen minutes to settle. I've been to a couple of performance trials, and I find that when hounds have a slower start we tend to have better runs."

I asked whether he felt that the performance trial was a fair test of a hound.

"I think the performance trial is a *very* fair test of a hound," he said. "The top hounds always come shining through. But the hounds that are more marginal—good, decent hounds—will really accelerate being packed with so many top hounds. They feed off each other."

That was an interesting observation, but I wondered if it had a lasting effect.

"It does," said Brown. "My hounds have always come home and hunted better for the next few weeks—sharper, keener, more aware, more apt to listen, even more thorough going through a covert. In this trial you had eight packs that brought five of their best hounds each. There wasn't a stone that went unturned! I think that's what steps up the marginal hounds."

I asked Michael what it was like for a huntsman who hunts the fox at home to come to Georgia and hunt the coyote.

"It's like pouring gasoline on the fire!" Brown answered.

Although Midland Crystal 2002 turned in the winning performance overall, Belle Meade won the pack standings with two hounds—
Whiskey and Jack—racking up the points.

"We sweated over our selections for this trial," Master Epp Wilson
said. "We tried to pick the rising stars that will peak in the Centennial
year. Whiskey is a small hound. He's like Avis car rental—always
number two—so he tries harder. Jack is a young hound that gets to
the front more easily and casts wider. We also considered the 'kinder-
garten factor' in our selections. You know—plays well with others.
We wanted hounds that would enter well to a strange pack."

CENTENNIAL TRIALS: 2006/2007

Thirteen Centennial Performance Trials were held over the period
from October 2006 to October 2007, hosted by Fox River Valley
Hunt (IL), Wayne-duPage Hunt (IL), London Hunt and Toronto and
North York Hunt (ON), Millbrook Hunt (NY), Moore County
Hounds and Sedgefield Hunt (NC), Green Spring Valley Hounds and
Elkridge-Harford Hunt (MD), Aiken Hounds (SC), Belle Meade
Hunt (GA), West Hills Hunt (CA), Harvard Foxhounds (OK), Coal
Valley Hounds (KS), Arapahoe Hunt (CO), and Rappahannock and
Bull Run Hunts (VA).

The top ten scoring hounds of each Centennial Performance
Trial earned the title of Centennial Foxhound for that event. The top
five hounds in each trial earned the national title of Centennial
Champion Foxhound.

Moore County Hounds/Sedgefield Hunt

Masters, staff, and members of the Moore County Hounds had already
provided more than a week of sport and hospitality even before the
performance trials—the concluding events of Carolinas Hunt Week—
began. Nine days of Centennial Joint Meets, art show, hunter pace,
trail ride, driving exhibition, hunt ball, breakfasts, and dinner parties
preceded the final event.

The first day's meeting of performance trial hounds was held in
the J. Robert Gordon Field Trial Grounds near Southern Pines—an
excellent nine-thousand-acre bird dog field trial venue, featuring
clubhouse, stabling, and kenneling facilities. Unfortunately, the
grounds had been used for bird dog trials on each of the six previous
days, and foxes were scarce by the time the foxhounds arrived. The
second day's hunting was held in the renowned Walthour-Moss Foundation area—the principal hunting country for the Moore County
Hounds—where a good hunt developed late in the day. Hounds were
scored well and often.

Flat Branch Foxhounds (NC) made an exceptionally impressive
showing. That hunt brought only two hounds to the trial—Falstaff and
Finesse. Falstaff was high scorer for the trial, and Finesse finished third.

Falstaff 2003, a Crossbred dog hound (entered to hunting by Why
Worry Hounds), was always trying, always among the leaders, always
doing the hard work. On the final good run of the day, when hounds
were at fault, I watched him recover the line on his own and set the
pack straight and running again. Here's what it sounded like on my
tape recorder back at the judge's meeting:

11:25, *hunting*, number 59 . . . 81 . . . 20.
(hound speaks)
20 *trailing*! 20 is trailing.
(The voice of huntsman Leahy from a distance)
"Norman, score that dog, 20!"
"Yeah, I got him."
(Leahy doubles his horn.)

"Falstaff was the most powerful dog there late in the day," said
Tony Leahy, trial huntsman. "He did a beautiful job on that coyote."

Leahy also had praise for some Moore County hounds and a Red
Mountain dog on that particular run.

"They did well, but they were way behind," he said. "It was a
tough scenting day in a tough scenting country, and the other good
hounds just got left."

Centennial Trials Conclude in Virginia

"We finally pulled it off," said Rappahannock MFH Oliver Brown.

Brown was referring to the Centennial Foxhound Performance Trial, originally scheduled to be held last March, but postponed due to an equine infection that shut down all horse sports in Virginia for nearly a month. Rappahannock Hunt Masters Brown, Janet O'Keefe, and Gus Edwards, and Bull Run Hunt Masters Joe Kincheloe, John Smith, and Travis White plus members of both hunts collaborated to stage this, the final Trial in the Centennial series.

The first day's hunting was hosted by Rappahannock at their excellent fixture, Larry Levy's "The Hill." Trial huntsman Tony Leahy drew the coverts in a clockwise direction, and even I (perpetually lost in the country) could go off alone on my quest to score hounds and still find my way back before dark. The entire fixture comprises fewer than four hundred acres, but with its folding hills, coverts, and running water, a whole day's hunting may be had there.

"What struck me about the first day," commented Jake Carle, ex-MFH, "and it was a pattern that repeated itself over and over, hounds jumped foxes up on the ridges and they'd run right down to Devil's Run where the fog was lying so heavy, and it killed scent completely. Hounds threw their heads up, and that was it."

Later in the morning, the wind came up, the fog lifted, and hounds had two good runs—the last one by the "toilet jump."

Carle explains: "Larry Levy had cleaned out some old houses, and he had a whole bunch of toilets to throw away. Well, they wanted $13.00 apiece to take them to the dump, so he said, 'The hell with you.' He filled them with dirt, put them in with a bunch of old tires, piled dirt on them, and made a jump! It's claimed a few riders."

I remember passing that substantial earthen obstacle and was just as happy to keep on going.

The second day's hunting, hosted by the Bull Run Hunt, was held at Mike Long's beautiful property, The Preserve. Bull Run huntsman Greg Schwartz guided Leahy over this extensive, magnificent open country. Hounds found several gray foxes in the first covert. However, the weather had remained hot and dry, and scenting conditions were again difficult.

"One huge gray strolled right out in front of Mike and Charlie and Oliver Brown, glanced at them without concern, and just walked into another cornfield," said Carle.

Hounds then trailed a fox pretty well up onto Cedar Mountain, but couldn't own the line. It was a moving experience to ride over this, the scene of the famous Civil War battle involving General Pope for the Union and Generals Stonewall Jackson and A. P. Hill for the Confederates. The battle ended in favor of the Confederates in 1862 and in favor of the fox in 2007.

25

A CENTENNIAL CELEBRATION IN THE PACIFIC SOUTHWEST

Red Rock Hounds Host Centennial Joint Meet

2007

Consider for a moment the entire body of literature inspired by mounted fox-hunting. It embraces a time span of about two hundred years and has been limited for most of that period to stories—however well-written and enjoyed—of foxhunting as practiced in England, Ireland, and the North American east.

Well, the foxhunting world is really bigger than that. In the last fifteen years, MFHA Executive Director Dennis Foster has opened our eyes and our imagination with his stories of mounted hunting as practiced in Australia and New Zealand. And with this story, we go to the high desert of Nevada where cowboys in dusty western hats, vests, and chaps lope after hounds in their Western saddles stirrup-to-stirrup with properly attired foxhunters posting to the trot in their English saddles.

When I was a child I had a favorite aunt whose stories of her everyday adventures were either hilarious or horrendous but never mundane. She lived on another planet where everything happened in excess.

One day I was over the moon with one of her stories, and my father brought me down to earth. "Listen," he told me privately, "divide whatever she tells you by three, and you'll be closer to the facts."

It wasn't until many years later that I discovered my father was wrong. Some people's worlds *are*, in fact, magnified from reality.

My first proof of that was when I went foxhunting in Ireland. There, the most improbable and impossible things happen routinely. You come home and tell the stories, and no one believes you. Yet they're all true!

Certain people are like that, too. Take Lynn Lloyd. How many Masters can spin you a yarn about their entire pack of hounds swimming in pursuit of a duck in a pond for over an hour in full cry? And follow that story up with a place she knows where hounds draw past a prickle* of porcupines—hundreds of them—staring with beady little eyes from bushes and tree branches as you pass by. This is the woman who, on a trip across the country in 1980, ran out of gas in Reno, Nevada, stayed, and started the Red Rock Hounds.

This is the same woman who, some years earlier, traveled from the East Coast to the West Coast on horseback, alone. She endured drenching rains and snow. She faced down three Mexican bandits who tried to steal her water and horses on the desert. She robbed a moving train of three jerricans of water when she ran out of water on the desert. She saved a man's life. She made lasting friends of many people who took her in during her journey or gave her shelter. And there were those who wouldn't help when tornadoes were bearing down even though it would have cost them nothing. She bathed in freezing streams, ate one-can meals of fruit or spinach, then made cowboy coffee (she calls it *cowgirl* coffee) in the empty can. Much of the time she slept under the stars. She stopped and worked for a week at a big feedlot out west and gained the admiration of the hard-bitten cowboys there. They presented her with a beautiful pair of Tony Lama boots when she left. She figured out how to keep her horses sound, how to pack her pack horse, and how to keep her dog from wearing out the pads of his feet just by going out and *doing* it.

---

*Collectively, cows graze in a *herd*; fish swim in a *school*; and porcupines hang out together in a *prickle*!

Red Rock Hounds MFH Lynn Lloyd hunts the high desert of Nevada, a country as vast as her own spirit.   *Kathy Tourney photo*

Welcome to the world of Lynn Lloyd, an improbable planet suited only to inhabitants who are themselves larger than life. Even the country she hunts mirrors the scale and scope of her spirit. I had heard about it, but until you see it on horseback, the sheer vastness cannot be appreciated. But I'm getting ahead of myself.

CENTENNIAL JOINT MEET IN THE HIGH DESERT

The Pacific District Centennial Joint Meet was hosted by Lynn Lloyd's Red Rock Hounds from October 2 to October 7 near Reno, Nevada (elevation around 4,400 feet). Reno is located upon a broad valley plain in the Sierra Nevada range of mountains that extends northwesterly-southeasterly through much of eastern California, with just a small portion of the eastern foothills touching Nevada and the Red Rock country.

The celebration consisted of four days of hunting, hunt breakfasts, dinner parties, and a book signing by best-selling author Rita Mae Brown, MFH. Seven hunts from the Western District participated, and Masters and foxhunters from Colorado, Florida, Kansas, New Jersey, New York, Oklahoma, Ontario, and Virginia joined in the fun (see sidebar).

Now, having actually ridden over the country for the first time, I can say I finally appreciate what those old Western movies were *really* about. Water and dust.

In the great American Southwest, water is king. Whoever controls the water controls his own future and the fortunes of all the others who depend on his water. That's what all those Western movie range wars were about. Remember?

Also, I came to appreciate how easily the Indians spotted the westbound settlers crossing the country. Dust. Clouds of it. Churned up by anything that moves. Including a pack of foxhounds racing after a coyote. Or bobcat. Or mountain lion.

Foxhounds would also love to run the jackrabbits with the impossibly huge ears that jump up out of the sagebrush right under their

WIDESPREAD SUPPORT FOR PACIFIC DISTRICT CENTENNIAL JOINT MEET

Four hunts from the Pacific District and one hunt from the Rocky Mountain District brought hounds:

- Red Rock Hounds (NV): MFHs Gayle Horn, Lynn Lloyd, and Scott Tepper
- Santa Fe Hunt (CA): Terry Paine, MFH
- West Hills Hounds (CA): MFHs Mitch Jacobs, Scott Tepper, and Mike Zacha
- Woodbrook Hunt (WA): MFHs Jean Brooks and Mike Wager
- Grand Canyon Hounds (AZ): MFHs Paul Delaney and Stephania Williams

Masters from many hunts across North America participated:

- MFHs Keith and Melinda Baxter and Katie Graham, Los Altos Hounds (CA)
- Mack Braly, MFH, Harvard Fox Hounds (OK)
- Dr. Rita Mae Brown, MFH, Oak Ridge Fox Hounds (VA)
- Cathy Kornacki, MFH, Fort Leavenworth Hunt (KS)
- Steve Lyons, MFH, Santa Ynez Valley Hounds (CA)
- Alexis and Mac Macaulay, MFHs, Misty Morning Hounds (FL)

Beagle and Harrier packs were represented:

- John Auborn, MH, Kingsbury Harriers
- Jim Beisel, MB, Settlers Acre Beagles
- Margaret Bohannon and Suzie Stevenson, MBs, Paradise Valley Beagles

Statistics: One hundred fifty-five foxhunters from all parts of the country registered to ride. Many were accompanied by nonriding spouses and guests. Forty horses were leased to visitors.

noses. Although Master and huntsman Lynn Lloyd likes to see them, because there is often a coyote close by, she doesn't consider jackrabbits worthy of her hounds' attention, and she stops them.

I had the opportunity to ride up with Lynn and watch hounds work. Red Rock, Santa Fe, and Woodbrook hounds made up the pack of forty couple on the first day. Although there were hounds of all colors in the mixed pack, Lynn, whose Red Rock pack is based on Treeing Walker bloodlines, tries to breed tricolor hounds for visibility in all kinds of terrain and weather, especially snow. Foxhunters at Red Rock wait for and welcome the snow that furnishes the blessed moisture.

On this day, however, hounds labored under warm, dry, and dusty conditions, but never stopped trying. They spread out widely in front of their huntsman with whippers-in on the flanks as far as a mile away, looking like ants in the distance. Coyotes were viewed and run briefly, but hounds inhaled mostly dust and windblown grit rather than the lovely scent they dearly wanted.

The country is enormous. At one point we stood on the top of a rock-strewn hill as Lynn called hounds to her. We looked *down* upon birds soaring over the valley below us. The immediate field of view, which consisted of the stretch of valley and the mountains opposite rising three thousand feet from the valley floor, all within reach, probably encompassed thirty thousand acres of nothing but sagebrush, greasewood bushes, and, in places, a few stunted junipers. Nothing moved. In the course of the entire first day's hunting, in all of this government-owned and -managed open rangeland, I saw only two head of cattle grazing. (The United States government owns 87 percent of the entire landmass of Nevada, and the Bureau of Land Management [BLM] administers 67 percent of Nevada's landmass.)

On the second day, Grand Canyon huntsman Peter Wilson hunted ten couple of his hounds from the Campbell Springs fixture. Hounds drew well, moving actively ahead of their huntsman, and, despite similar conditions to the previous day, a couple of short hunts were enjoyed. On a historical note, Campbell Springs is the site of the last Indian massacres in the country (1905).

"GENTLEMEN, WE'RE RICH"

After the second day's hunting, on Thursday night, a special dinner party was hosted by Red Rock member and honorary whipper-in [now Joint-Master] John Schaefer. It was special for many reasons, first, perhaps, because of the location—Virginia City—which is tucked away, high out of sight, several thousand feet above Reno and the valley floor, in the Virginia Range of the Sierras.

One drives, climbing steadily, over twelve miles of winding switch-backs to reach this nineteenth-century town that still looks like a Hollywood set for a Western movie. In the mid-1800s, the "Forty-Niners" were digging for gold there and paving the streets with the blue-gray mud that kept clogging their extraction equipment. One day in 1857 a mine owner returned from the arduous trip to the assay office.

"Gentlemen, we're rich," he told his partners.

The blue-gray mud with which they had been paving the roads was almost pure silver. They had struck what would become known as the Comstock Lode.

Schaefer lives in a stately old home furnished with lovely antiques at the edge of Virginia City. He seated one hundred fifty guests for dinner, and, before sending them home, entertained them with a performance of songs, complete with piano accompaniment, worthy of a Broadway production.

The evening was special for a final reason: it snowed in the late hours, thus improving the sport for the next two days.

BLESSED MOISTURE

It wasn't a lot of snow, and it remained only in patches for the Saturday and Sunday meets, but the moisture it brought was enough to improve scenting conditions. On Saturday, Lynn hunted thirty-one couple of her own hounds. After a mile hack to the first "covert"—

the first hillside—hounds hit immediately and ran to the top of the mountain after two coyotes.

On Sunday, West Hills huntsman David Wendler hunted sixteen-and-a-half couple of the West Hills and Santa Fe hounds. Hounds struck and carried two lines for two hours, at speed, crossing several hills—almost mountains—and checked in the juniper-forested area of the Sand Hills. Wendler collected hounds, then found another coyote that carried them back to the meet.

After more than twenty-five years of hunting hounds in this vast country, Lynn Lloyd has acquired somewhat of a legendary status. However, it wasn't always that way. She was not welcomed with open arms by all the westerners. She brought an unfamiliar culture to the open range, and she used a lot of territory to practice it. Slowly, however, she gained the admiration of many. Santa Ynez Valley MFH Steve Lyons recalls an incident at the 1995 District Meet at Red Rock.

"All of a sudden a bunch of cowboys carrying shotguns came galloping over a rise.

"'Who the hell are you, and what are you doing here?' one demanded to know. 'You're trespassing.'

"Lynn said, 'We have the owner's permission to hunt coyote here. My name is Lynn Lloyd.'

"'You're the famous Lynn Lloyd?' The cowboy exclaimed. He dismounted, took off his hat, and dropped to his knees!"

The Red Rock Hounds went hunting.

Scott J. Tepper, MFH of the Red Rock Hounds and the West Hills Hunt, contributed to this story.

26

OH, THOSE MIDLAND HOUNDS!

2007

Another October; another MFHA fall directors meeting. In 2007, President Mason Lampton, MFH of the Midland Fox Hounds, invited officers and directors to meet and hunt in his Fitzpatrick, Alabama, country.

The occasion also happened to coincide with Lampton's birthday, and he and Mary Lu threw the biggest costume party I've ever seen. I went as a foreign correspondent.

Fitzpatrick, Alabama: a sportsman's paradise of game-filled wooded coverts, open fields for cattle grazing, and clayey moisture-holding turf they call prairie gumbo. Flawless morning sky, gentle air, the bustle of trailers parking, friends greeting, an army of visitors climbing aboard strange horses. Suddenly, the sound of a chopper.

It comes into view over the trees and, in a fluid combination of maneuvers, banks rakishly, executes a turn on the forehand, sideslips like a dancer; drops, hovers, and settles as gently as you would put a baby in the crib. Field member Dr. Phil Beegle, I'm told, found himself with so much time on his hands while attending medical school that he decided to learn to fly a helicopter. Today is the Opening Meet of the Midland Fox Hounds.

Stirrup Cup, ham biscuits, the Blessing of Hounds, and Master and huntsman Mason Lampton, host to this field of 125 riders and nearly as many friends on foot, sends hounds into the first covert—nearly in sight of the meet.

The entire pack erupts at once, every hound with something important to say, and this legendary pack of Crossbred foxhounds is down to business with one thought in mind—putting its quarry *out* of business.

A visitor on a strange horse in Midland's coyote country, hardly settled in the saddle yet, and I'm anticipating the headlong rush of a long, hard coyote run. But it's stop, double back, forward, and double back again. Feels like gray fox. Lampton says later that, although he didn't see it, gray fox have been seen in the area.

Hounds pressure this gray long enough for me to quickly realize that this is my lucky day. It's always a question mark with a strange horse until you're over the first fence, but today I have a winner: Todd, the family favorite of Mooreland Master Leslie Rhett Crosby. Steady, athletic, and smooth, the fences are just another stride to Todd. I switch to autopilot and turn my attention to the hounds.

At the checks, two things strike me at once: every hound in the pack works actively and energetically to recover the line, and every hound that finds a shred of scent speaks with confidence and urgency.

"Here, over here! No, I've got it here! No, come on and help me; this is really it!"

Hounds run the gray fox to ground in a brushpile and mark it well. A coyote is viewed away, but hounds find another. With a high blue sky, low humidity and an east wind, hounds are having difficulty really owning the line. They work hard and speak enthusiastically, but are brought to their noses time and again.

"We were walking the game to boredom," complained Lampton afterward.

Although everyone in the field seemed to think we were having a good day, it wasn't until later that Lampton got what he was hoping for.

"The last run started along a stream, and the pace quickly became furious," he recalled. "The coyote must have been very close when they first scented him. Even then, as all day, they struggled in the woods. He broke out of the woods and was viewed by Jack McDonald [MFH, London Hunt (ON)] and Jamie Redmond, who gave a world-class

Romping over the grass at the Midland opening meet are (left to right): Daphne Wood, MFH and past president of the MFHA; Dr. George Seier, editor of the current edition of the *Foxhound Kennel Notebook*; and Rene Latiolais, past MFHA Centennial Chairman and current Secretary-Treasurer of the MFHA. *Curtis Robb photo*

holloa! I lifted the hounds to the view, and the scent must have been sizzling. They went away like a flight of teal with a roaring cry."

Hounds ran for an hour, covering many more miles, after they had already given the field a good three hours.

"They exhibited what we adore—extreme intensity with a cry that hit every note to create a true symphony," said Lampton. "The day had been fun, but the last run gave us the rush of a jet engine. We had to stop, but it was a lovely exhibition of what the Midland hounds can do."

27

GOLDEN'S BRIDGE

Small Country, Big Sport

2008

I met Ed Kelly, MFH of the Golden's Bridge Hounds (NY), after he was elected to serve as director of the New York/New Jersey District of the MFHA. Since moving to Virginia from my native Massachusetts many years ago, I have never sought opportunities to return to those colder northern climes during the hunting season. On this occasion, however, I was very happy to have done so.

On a bright, cool day following the Golden's Bridge Hounds, not forty-five miles from New York City, I watched as several of foxhunting's conventional wisdoms were demolished.

Penn-Marydels are slow. Well, I saw this pack run down a coyote in the open. The pack was running so tightly, it took a moment for me to realize that the lead hound was, in fact, the coyote. One hound rolled it, but it managed to escape with its brush. A very lucky coyote, that one.

Penn-Marydels dwell. OK, so the line is their religion. But the huntsman can compensate for this tendency and get them forward, as Ciaran Murphy did so well this day. As we've noted before on these pages, Penn-Marydels can run; it's all in the way they're handled in the field.

You need big, open country to hunt coyote. The hunting country this day consisted of no more than eight hundred acres, including Master

Eugene Colley's Windswept Farm, the site of the meet. True, we jumped some of the same fences in both directions several times during the course of the day, but it's also true that hounds ran three foxes and a coyote through this fixture and didn't even use all of it in three-and-a-half hours of hunting.

You need Thoroughbred horses when you're chasing coyote. All I can tell you is that Dennis Foster and I returned home with puncture wounds in each of our two Thoroughbreds, while the rugged draft crosses seemed to make their way through the trappy places unscathed. And, in this tighter country, the warmbloods are able to keep up with hounds perfectly well.

The Golden's Bridge country consists of grassy fields in the higher places, wooded rides in the middle ground, and rocks and boggy places in the low spots—in short, good, foxy country. We viewed the first fox crossing the grass and followed hounds as he took them down

Huntsman Ciaran Murphy "makes the day adventurous" for the Golden's Bridge field. From right to left: Murphy and MFHs Ken Silverman, Ed Kelly, and Bruce Colley. *Jim Duggan photo*

The coyote was run down in the open by the Golden's Bridge Penn-Marydels and rolled over by the lead hound, but managed to escape unscathed. *Jim Duggan photo*

to the lower, thicker places. Field Master Ed Kelly kept us well abreast of the pack on a well-maintained network of trails, as hounds raced through the trees after their fox. Mixed with the wind in our ears were the deep, throaty baritones of the Penn-Marydels filling the woods with their joy.

MFHA Executive Director Dennis Foster rode up with huntsman Ciaran Murphy and was in a good position to watch the pack work.

"Ciaran did an exceptional job," said Foster. "He knew when to leave hounds alone and when to give them some help. He showed great patience in letting them work in the slews, and he was very good at using all the country he has."

Irish-born Murphy, a graduate of the MFHA's new Hunt Staff Apprentice Program, came to Golden's Bridge as huntsman four years ago. His predecessor, Donald Philhower (who now hunts the Mill-brook foxhounds a bit farther north), is a highly experienced, long-time breeder of Penn-Marydel foxhounds and had shared bloodlines over the years with Jody Murtagh, ex-MFH of the Rose Tree (PA) and current huntsman of the Moore County Hounds (SC). The pack is now probably half Philhower's breeding and half Murphy's.

"We've been really pleased with Ciaran's ability to hunt the coverts thoroughly," Master Ed Kelly said. "One of the foxes was found today because of his thoroughness."

Kelly keeps his field close to Murphy and the hounds.

"I recently heard someone describe hunting as an adventure on horseback," recalled Kelly. "We have a very enthusiastic field that likes to be with hounds. Ciaran makes the day adventurous, and we keep up!"

～ 28 ～

YOUNG HUNTSMAN SHOWS GOOD SPORT—WITH STYLE— AT CAMDEN

2008

I was in Aiken, South Carolina, enjoying the special ambiance of that charming town—the benign climate, the excellent footing for my horse, old friends, the lovely Hitchcock Woods, and the hunting. With four established hunt clubs, Aiken is a wonderful place for northern-based foxhunters to escape the winter doldrums. However, since one of our favorite contributors, Betsy Parker, had recently written an article for Covertside *on that very scene, I had to look elsewhere for material.*

That was easy. Just a one-and-a-half-hour drive from Aiken is Camden, South Carolina—an old, well-established equestrian community that has attracted horsemen and horsewomen from many equestrian disciplines for more than a hundred years. I had never been there, but I knew the young professional huntsman at the Camden Hunt from his earlier years as an amateur whipper-in. It was a great opportunity to see both a young huntsman and a venerable hunt, each for the first time, so my traveling buddy and I made arrangements for a day's hunting.

Good sport is what all huntsmen strive for, but when good sport is executed with class . . . panache . . . polish . . . that's the icing on the cake. That's what's happening in Camden, South Carolina, and it's a delight to see. A young huntsman there—Chad Wilkes—is showing sport with style and confidence well beyond his years.

"We're lucky to have him," said Sandy Cushman, MFH, "but he's lucky to be here as well. We're a laid-back hunt, and we don't put a lot of pressure on a young huntsman. Chad has the freedom to try different things and develop his skills. And we love his youth and enthusiasm."

Wilkes grew up hunting, then whipping-in as an amateur to Epp Wilson, MFH and huntsman of the Belle Meade Hunt in nearby Georgia. Wilkes's father, Dr. Gary Wilkes, is a Joint-Master at Belle Meade. From Belle Meade, young Wilkes went first to the Hard Away Hounds (now Hard Away Whitworth Hounds) in Alabama as a professional huntsman for the 2004/2005 season, then to the Camden Hunt the following season.

I had known Wilkes at Belle Meade and wanted to catch up with him in his current duties. A friend, Jef Murdock, and I drove over to the Camden kennels from Aiken, where we were visiting, to have a day with hounds.

TOWN AND COUNTRY

Camden, the oldest inland city in South Carolina, was established by King George II in 1730 as Fredericksburg. It was renamed in honor of Lord Camden, a champion of colonial rights. During the Revolutionary War, British General Cornwallis occupied Camden in 1780 with twenty-five hundred troops and on August 17 handed the Americans their worst defeat of the entire war. However, the following year, Revolutionary General Nathaniel Greene confronted a British force there, and, despite losing the battle, made it so costly for the Redcoats that they left Camden.

In the late 1800s Camden became a winter destination for wealthy northern families. Equestrian activities, especially polo, grew quickly. The Camden Hunt was founded in 1926, and the Carolina Cup was inaugurated four years later. A South Carolina steeplechasing tradition,

Huntsman Chad Wilkes shows sport with a style and confidence beyond his years.
Catherine French photo

the race now draws crowds of more than seventy-five thousand spectators each spring.

The Camden Hunt has access to approximately ten thousand contiguous acres—their primary hunting territory—where the kennels and hunt barn are situated. Owned by the Thiel family (Judith Thiel is the senior Master) and by Mrs. Richard Lloyd, the area has been placed in conservation for foxhunting and other equine activities. This day's meet was at the kennels, and the area hunted is referred to locally as the Carolina Bays, where gray foxes are found in the lower, thicker parts and coyotes in the higher, more open woods.

The Carolina Bays are fascinating geological phenomena distributed along the Atlantic coastal plain from Delaware to Florida, characterized by elliptical depressions of anywhere from one to several thousand acres in size. There are perhaps five hundred thousand of these depressions up and down the coast, often clustered in groups, the long axes of the ellipses usually aligned in a northwest-southeast direction. Some contain water, some are marshy, while others contain thick vegetation—good places to seek the gray fox!

The footing is sand, typical of the Carolinas. The country is mostly wooded—pine and scrub oaks—and trails are cut and maintained throughout. Although the country is unfenced and jumping is not necessary to stay with hounds, a variety of hunt jumps—coops, Aikens, rails, logs—have been built across the trails for sport, with "go-arounds" for the second field. No gates! The fences are inviting and positioned on the wide, sandy trails to be taken at a rhythmic hand gallop—no queuing up here!

DRAWING THE CAROLINA BAYS

Trotting to the first draw, it was clear that Wilkes has a special rapport with his hounds. The pack, consisting mainly of Hardaway Crossbreds—mostly three-quarter English, a few full English—was attentive and obedient. Wilkes brings them along a bit more loosely than many English huntsmen would be comfortable with, but no corrections were required as we hacked on down the trails. In fact, it didn't appear that whippers-in were needed to help with hounds at all. Joint-Masters Sandy Cushman and Dan Floyd rode out on compass flanks, mostly out of sight, primarily as spotters and to help if needed.

And here is something the Camden Masters might not want advertised too broadly, but if you like to ride up close to hounds while hunting, this is the place. In fact, although the first field had an excellent Field Master this day in Susan Provenzano, truly, Chad Wilkes is both the huntsman *and* the Field Master at Camden. Provenzano and her field ride no more than a few horse's lengths behind him, close enough in fact so that field members often find themselves in the midst of hounds, within clear earshot of Wilkes's occasional commentary provided for their benefit.

"These hounds are so used to running coyote, they tend to overrun the line of a gray fox," Wilkes complained as hounds checked after finding and running but a short distance.

Scenting, in fact, was difficult this day, and the dry oak leaves that continue to fall from the trees all winter long don't help the scenting conditions in this sandy, well-drained country. Nevertheless, Wilkes is a very quiet and patient huntsman. He uses his horn only sparingly, relying mostly on his voice and the occasional whistle to let hounds know where he is. He switches into a traditional huntsman's tenor to express encouragement, using words that are totally unintelligible to us, as well they ought to be!

When hounds find and speak, Wilkes remains silent, allowing his hounds to work it out and settle to the line without distractions from him. Hounds accept their responsibility and fly to each other to honor the one that is speaking.

Wilkes shook his head in frustration. "See how hounds are running the line well for just a short distance, then losing the scent," he said. "Other huntsmen in the area have been complaining of the same problem. We don't know why."

Picking up hounds, Wilkes continued to keep the field informed.

"Let's see if we can find a coyote," he said.

Sometimes the coyote can get you in trouble. For a day that started fairly sedately, it ended with a bit more excitement than Wilkes might have wished for.

Hounds found their coyote, and it was pure pleasure to fall into a comfortable hand gallop along the sandy trails, taking the inviting fences in stride without breaking rhythm, no concerns about ground-hog holes, all the while staying well in touch with the pack, indeed, often finding ourselves galloping alongside the pack, close to the music, as they flew through the pines.

Presently the field, close as we were, had a wonderful view of our dark-hued pilot who streaked away across the first large expanse of grass I had seen. The grass, however, turned out to be the edge of a commercial airfield adjacent to U.S. Route 1, and hounds, unmindful of airport or highway, raced after their quarry, as did Wilkes and the field.

Next came a flurry of radio transmissions from the road whips advising that coyote and hounds had crossed busy U.S. Route 1, but they were there stopping traffic and had matters under control. Wilkes raced across the airfield, with the field in his wake. Behind us, a jet that had been warming up took off down the runway.

The coyote had known just where the chain-link fence separating the airfield from the road ended, and had taken half the pack across the busy road. It was a miracle that no hounds were injured and no accident occurred. My enduring image of this day will forever be that of Chad Wilkes kneeling in the middle of U.S. Route 1, blowing his horn—eighteen wheelers, oil tankers, buses, and automobiles at a dead stop in both directions—embracing hounds one by one as they returned to him. Magically, Wilkes's wife, Melissa, had also appeared, summoned from her office, to catch the last hound—one they raised—who they knew would be shy of all the commotion and strangers. As the field stood waiting on the airport grass, field member Kathy Stahl turned to me.

"If I wind up in jail, can I get *Covertside* forwarded to my new address?" she asked.

29

FOXHUNTERS ON SAFARI

2008

What does an African safari have to do with foxhunting? I asked myself that question when foxhunter Heidi Beaumont invited me to go on a riding safari in Kenya and write an article for Covertside.

Heidi is a travel specialist who packages African horseback safaris through her company International Ventures, Ltd. She had asked her friend Jeannie Thomas, MFH of the Why Worry Hounds (SC), to recommend someone to do it, and Jeannie, bless her, suggested me.

According to Heidi, the riding safari was very popular with foxhunters, and in thinking about it I began to see the parallels: the love of wildlife in its natural setting; sitting on a horse in the wide open spaces; and a measure of risk. It turned out to be one of the great adventures of my life.

Ten horsemen stood on the bank of the Mara River under the midday equatorial sun as Tristan explained the crossing.

"We must cross here and land on the far bank at that tree, you see. You must point your horse upstream so the current doesn't carry you down to the hippos there."

A half dozen hippopotamuses—a species that kills more people in Africa than any other animal—alternately submerged, surfaced, snorted as they watched us not twenty-five yards downstream of our ideal route. A pair of ducks paddling furiously were carried rapidly downstream as we watched. A single, large male hippo broke the surface just upstream.

We would be surrounded, while our horses would struggle over the rocky bottom, water over the saddle flaps. We exchanged glances, each of us holding to our own thoughts. I moved forward—get in and get it over with—my way of dealing with apprehension.

Not five minutes earlier, as we approached the river, our little band of horsemen happened by a safari vehicle carrying tourists safely inside. Several faces peered out at us curiously, and we sat tall in our saddles. The difference between a safari on horseback and a safari by vehicle has to be the difference between a warm embrace and a handshake. On horseback we are directly in touch with the earth. We walk over the animal tracks, the bleached bones, the lumps of elephant dung, the eons-old volcanic rocks in our path. We inhale the scents of nature, not diesel fumes. We hear the myriad unfamiliar bird calls instead of the engine's roar. We are dancing to the rhythm of our horses' footfalls rather than the random jostle of the all-terrain vehicle. All such feelings of superiority had vanished, however, as we stood on the riverbank trying to gauge the mood of the hippos.

Tristan led the way down, and we followed in single file. Once in the water, where a fast escape was impossible, our heads swiveled from side to side monitoring the hippos. The water leaking into my boots felt curiously cool and comforting. The good news was that we all made it safely across; the bad news was that we learned we would have to recross the river a couple of days later.

It had all started with an e-mail from Heidi Beaumont, a foxhunter I met while visiting with George and Jeannie Thomas's Why Worry Hounds in Aiken last year. Heidi runs International Ventures, Ltd., and specializes in organizing safaris in eastern and southern Africa. I learned that many of her clients for horseback safaris were fox-hunters, and I was anxious to discover the common ground for my-self. Heidi arranged for this, my first-ever African safari, with Offbeat Safaris in Kenya, run by the husband and wife team of Tristan and Cindy Voorspuy.

OUR LITTLE BAND

In addition to Tristan, there were nine other riders in our little band: two more American foxhunters in addition to me, Angela Royal from the Red Mountain Foxhounds in North Carolina and John Huganir from the Rose Tree Foxhunting Club in Pennsylvania; John Romero, a trail rider from California; three Frenchmen, Bertrand Devillars, Philippe Pascal, and Loïc le Masne de Chermont, who brought with them several bottles of exquisite wine and enormous senses of humor; and two of Tristan's friends, Derek de la Harpe, a tourism and wildlife consultant from South Africa, and Garth Thompson, professional guide, author, naturalist, and brilliant photographer from Zimbabwe. All photographs used in this article were taken by Garth and Derek on this safari.

Garth has guided people by canoe and on foot on photographic safaris in southern Africa for twenty-nine years. However, "Here," he admitted, "is the greatest wildlife spectacle in the world."

Garth loves the riding safari.

"It's the greatest thing in the world to be able to cover the country on the back of an animal you have a natural affinity for and watch all the wildlife around you," he said.

THE HORSEBACK SAFARI

The horseback safari experience is relatively recent. In 1984, English-born Tristan Voorspuy went to work for Tony Church, who owned and ran Safaris Unlimited. Tony was the first to introduce riding safaris in Kenya in 1972. Tony's son Gordon now manages that company. In 1990, Tristan went off on his own and established Offbeat Safaris.

The Offbeat Safaris literature tells you up front that "you must be a good enough rider to be able to gallop out of danger." That is a statement not to be ignored, for Tristan caters to the more adventuresome traveler.

"Adventuresome. Yes, I suppose that's what we have a reputation

With hippos watching us from both sides, we cross the Mara River.   *Garth Thompson photo*

for," Tristan agrees. "But I don't court disaster. You'll see our setup at Deloraine, where we have our own polo ground and cross-country schooling course. We spend a lot of time and effort on the horses. They play polo; they event; we work through the mistakes; we find out what they're good at."

The Voorspuys keep eighty horses at Deloraine, and Cindy—a brilliant horsewoman—does most of the schooling there. Tristan believes that when you have a reliable horse under you, and the footing is right, you can safely be more adventuresome. And he never misses

an opportunity for adventure. Trekking across the landscape, whenever he judged the footing favorable, he would stop and turn to us with a trace of a smile and a faraway look. That was the giveaway that he was ready for some excitement..

"Let's have a trot-canter."

That meant five strides at the trot followed by a two-mile hand gallop. If there was a herd of animals grazing, so much the better. We would find ourselves galloping as fast as the horses could go, with wildebeest, zebra, and gazelles galloping on both sides of us, wheeling

The author is entranced. For the horse, it's nothing unusual.   *Garth Thompson photo*

ahead, changing direction, splitting, reforming, drumming across the plain, a kaleidoscope of blurred motion, noise, and color.

Tristan can identify every animal, bird, and tree we pass, and his eyes are tuned to picking out and pointing out the smallest creatures well before anyone else can even see them. He and his staff take every opportunity to do more to make the adventure memorable than anyone could expect. There was a chair in front of my tent, ostensibly for sitting, reading, or relaxing, but I never had a moment to use it. A typical day began with an early game ride at sunrise, back for a full-course English breakfast, off again on horses or vehicles, lunch of cold cuts, cheeses, avocado salads at two, brief period for rest, afternoon ride at five until sunset, return for showers, cocktails, dinner, picture show of the previous day's photos, night game ride in the vehicles, bed at eleven.

FROM CAMP TO CAMP

Our first camp is Olare Lamun on the southern edge of the Loita Plains. On the very first game ride, the first full day in camp we ride past zebras, giraffes, wildebeest, impala, Thompson gazelles, Grant's gazelles, topi, hartebeest, dik-dik, baboons, warthogs, mongoose, jackal, aardvark, and hyenas. In the feathered category, we see the Batteleur Eagle, Long-Crested Eagle, Augur Buzzard, Superb Starling (looks like ours, but has a rose-colored breast and iridescent blue wings and back), Lilac-Breasted Roller, Egyptian Geese, among many others I never put names to. On a game ride in the vehicles after dinner, we view spring hare, white-tailed mongoose, and bat-eared fox, among other exotic creatures.

After two nights at Olare Lamun, we're up at six for breakfast, then break camp for our longest ride—about thirty miles—to the next camp, Olare Orok, at the edge of the Masai Game Reserve. Eleven riders spread out on the plain, including a groom with the extra horses—riding one, ponying one. The ponied horse is turned loose when we are far enough from Olare Lamun, and he follows.

We're crossing the country in the same way the early English settlers did a hundred years ago when they came to colonize Kenya. From the backs of our horses, we're seeing it just as they saw it. This is the bush; it hasn't been developed or "improved"; the Masai still build their brushy enclosures of acacia branches and huts of mud and dung. The men, draped in their colorful robes, tend their cattle, each holding his spear and his stick. Sun-bleached skeletons of animals long since passed are strewn over the Mara as they were then. There are some differences in our appointments, however: Derek has a portable GPS receiver tracking our route which he will later paste onto Google Earth for us; Angela has a minicam strapped to her hat brim; and others have international cell phones that communicate via satellite.

Soon we find ourselves galloping along with a herd of seventeen giraffes. They gallop in what looks like slow motion—a smoothly coordinated, rocking gait—but with their long legs they cover ground surprisingly swiftly.

We arrive at our rest stop at 1:30 p.m. in a small grassy bowl, by a stream surrounded by rocky outcroppings. We change to bathing suits and have a cool and refreshing dunk in the small ponds of water collected by the rock formations. Then a picnic lunch from our saddlebags.

All followed by a brief siesta under the tree. The only sounds are the tinkling of cow bells from a Masai herd grazing nearby.

On the horses and moving again at 3:00 p.m., we pass the bleached bones of an elephant that died, according to Tristan's estimate, in the early 1990s. We can still see the Loita Hills we left behind. Ahead we see the high escarpment marking the western edge of the Mara. To our left the hills in Tanzania are visible.

At 4:00 p.m. we top a rock ridge high above a breathtaking, broad and lush, flat valley colored in every hue of green and studded with small groves of trees. We take advantage of the good footing with a couple of long gallops across the valley floor.

I had been paranoid about the holes made by the aardvarks that dig for termites near the ubiquitous termite mounds, and find that I have been unnecessarily overcontrolling my horse. Today, I begin to see that my horse knows exactly where she wants to place each foot at all times. She sees or senses the holes and either avoids or leaps them. I succumb to her good sense and loosen the reins. She proves her point by galloping through a rocky place without touching a rock, with no guidance from me. I am reminded of Matthew Mackay-Smith's advice (*Covertside*, March 2008): the rider determines the direction and pace and leaves the gait and the placement of feet to the horse!

We arrive at Olare Orok, our camp at the edge of the Masai Game Reserve, just before 5:00 p.m. after seven-and-a-half hours in the saddle. We'll spend the next three nights here. The tents are already up, and the grooms are laying out the tarp onto which we will deposit saddles and bridles when we dismount.

The sun has set, and we are relaxing with predinner cocktails when a vehicle arrives to announce that a leopard has been seen. We pile into the vehicles for an evening game drive, bumping along in search of the leopard. With the help of the lamp we soon find her, hunting her way through the bush, a magnificent and healthy specimen. We savor for a short time our close encounter with this queen of beasts, then leave her to her quest.

The weather and temperature are perfect, so the dinner table has been set outside the dining tent in the open air. What emerges from the cooking tent, prepared over open fires and served by two of the staff in white jackets, would make any fine restaurant proud. Bread is baked fresh daily. After the soup course this night we have beef curry accompanied by a half-dozen bowls from which we can select a variety of chopped fruits, vegetables, and chutneys.

Later in my cot, tent zipped closed to keep out any wandering wildlife, I fall asleep to the night sounds of Africa—the ratchet and screech of the tree-dwelling bushbabies, the singsong of hyenas, the bark of baboons.

AN ANCIENT CULTURE, SCARCELY CHANGED

Much of the fertile Mara is owned by the Masai people. Past attempts by the various governments to coax them into a modern way of life have been generally unsuccessful, and they continue to live their seminomadic life in which wealth is measured by the number of cattle owned, and the important things in life—like the acquisition of wives—are paid for in cattle. Family groups build their own com- pounds—*manyattas*—which they enclose in an outer perimeter of thorny acacia branches interleaved to form a large ring. A smaller ring of brush inside contains the cattle at night. Between the two rings, in- dividual huts are built of mud, water, and cow or elephant dung packed between laths of sticks in the ground. There is no electricity or running water.

Tristan and other safari operators rent camp space from the local Masai. Tristan has established relationships with some of the Masai so that we were able to visit a compound, buy bracelets and trinkets di- rectly from the women, and even visit the inside of one of the huts. The floor was earthen. The first room opposite the entrance was for sheep, goats, or calves. Further into the smoky interior was the main room, quite bare, with a small fire burning. On each side of this room were two sleeping rooms—platforms, really—covered in skins.

A group of Masai men had danced for us in camp on a previous night as we sat by the campfire after dark. We cleared some space as they formed up outside of the ring of firelight. All was still. Then a rhythmic chanting. In formation, they come into the firelight stepping to the rhythm of their chant. One of the dancers tells the story in Masai, the others punctuate their chant with short shrills and cries. The dancers were exuberant and genuinely happy to demonstrate their skills, performing several dances, including the famous jumping steps for which they are renowned.

THE MATADOR AND THE ELEPHANT

Tristan and Cindy's second-in-command is a handsome twenty-eight-year-old from Argentina, Jacob von Plessen, who subscribes to Tristan's adventurous spirit entirely. During the winter, Jacob leads four or five riding safaris in Argentina, stressing a very comfortable camping experience similar to the African concept he has learned in Kenya.

Born in Austria, Jacob moved with his mother to Argentina at the age of three. He is fluent in five languages: English, French, German, Spanish, and Swahili.

"What brought you here?" I asked.

"I just think that third-world countries are far more interesting than developed countries," he replied. "Africa is a wonderful place. It comes with its disadvantages, but I think I'd rather choose a place like Africa with its disadvantages than a place like Europe with its advantages. There are beautiful places in Europe, but everything is so under control, so sterile.

"I live in the bush. That's my life now. But when I go on holidays, I go to the cities. I was in Europe for a month and a half on my last holiday, and I loved it—the culture, Vienna. My granny took me to museums and opera and all that, trying to civilize her wild little grandson."

Granny's wild little grandson, Jacob, was our guide on a couple of occasions when Tristan had other business to attend to. Here's how my diary recalls it:

We hear lions from our beds at about five this morning. Mounted at nine a.m. we've been riding for four hours at the top of the escarpment. Very different sort of terrain than where we have been—almost park-like—the sort of terrain that could be found in any country, even England. Very beautiful.

To reach the valley from our ridge, we dismount from the horses, change to rubber-soled walking shoes, and lead the horses on foot down a steep, narrow trail of rocks. The footing is treacherous; it would be impossible to ride horses down this trail. Jacob tells us that we must lead well ahead of the horses, and if one should lose its footing and fall, we must get out of the way quickly. The descent takes about twenty minutes, each footstep carefully chosen, leaping from one rock down to the next, but is accomplished without mishap.

Riding along the valley floor, we see a single large bull elephant. Jacob confronts it by walking slowly, one deliberate step at a time, toward the elephant. The elephant spreads its ears and puffs itself up so as to appear as large as possible. It is exceedingly large! Jacob continues to approach. I look behind me to find a nice, clean, open area for a galloping escape should the need arise. The elephant trumpets in anger and charges. Jacob's horse whirls, and he retreats until the elephant stops. Jacob resumes his advance, one step at a time. His adversary trumpets again and makes a mock charge. Jacob is no more than fifteen feet from the elephant, face to face, when the animal finally turns and slowly walks away. Jacob has faced down a wild bull elephant, just for kicks.

After about five-plus hours in the saddle, we are met by one of the vehicles and break for a lunch of sliced grilled sirloin cooked over an open fire by Jacob and accompanied by various salads. Siesta under a tree. The return ride will take about two-and-a-half hours, so we expect to get back around sunset.

On the way, we visit with large herds of Cape buffalo and gallop with the zebras. We hear the chinspot batis sing its signature descending three-note tune, "Three Blind Mice." We discover the water buck—a handsome antelope, medium dark brown, thickly furry, deerlike. He sports a bright, white hind end and is generally found near marsh or water.

What struck me powerfully about the animals I saw in Kenya was their superb state of health. Their coats are clean and sleek, their bellies full. Herbivores, carnivores, and scavengers—all living symbiotically on the plains as part of a complete and working ecosystem that has not yet been spoiled by man. It's all made possible by the particular geography and scale of the landscape. And by devoted naturalists like Tristan, Jacob, Garth, Derek, and others who have committed their lives to the preservation and enjoyment of these treasures.

30

THE RED MOUNTAIN WAY

2009

I visited the Red Mountain Foxhounds in Rougemont, North Carolina, for a reunion with friends—new and old—and a day of hunting. The new friend was my hostess, Angela Royal, whom I had met on safari in Kenya just a few months earlier. The old friend was Irmgard Hill, MFH of the Red Mountain, whom I knew from her years as a director of the MFHA during the early years of Covertside.

Unfortunately, the weather was uncooperative—a washout due to heavy rain—and hunting was canceled. However, I did enjoy a kennel tour and an illuminating interview with huntsman David Raley. In the course of that interview I saw and heard more evidence that the gentle Penn-Marydel foxhound may be an answer, especially in the future, to those hunts operating with smaller establishments, fewer paid professionals, and followers more interested in the pure chase than any eventual outcome.

English huntsmen might shake their heads, but David and his hounds do it their own way at Red Mountain.

I followed huntsman David Raley of the Red Mountain Hounds into kennels to see his pack of Penn-Marydels. Right away things looked a bit different. In most hunt kennels, dog hounds and bitches are confined to separate lodges. Here all the inside doors were open, and all hounds mixed freely.

"With the dogs and bitches mixed, we have no kennel fights," Raley explained.

Even the feeding is different at Red Mountain.

"I need to keep it simple and uncomplicated," he continued. "If I go away for a weekend, volunteers—members—have to cover for me. I feed free-choice food, and while hounds are eating, I pick up the kennels. I don't have to stand over them."

Raley explained that because feed is available to them for two to three hours, hounds aren't inclined to gulp it down or fight with their neighbors at the trough. Hounds that get too fat are drafted.

Admittedly the Penn-Marydel foxhound doesn't present the elegant image of the modern English or Crossbred hound—racy, streamlined, athletic, intense. But one look into their gentle brown eyes as they crowd around to greet you, and your heart melts for each and every one. They exude the friendly, laid-back attitude of the country hound lying under the porch, in contrast to the on-your-toes ambition of their high-church brothers and sisters.

One of the fascinating aspects of our hunting world is how each hunt develops its own culture. This uniqueness derives from a combination of factors, among them hunting country, history, community, personalities, and hunt organization. With hilly and wooded hunting terrain, honorary whippers-in recruited from the membership, and strictly volunteer help available for training and exercising, Penn-Marydels are the answer for Raley, who is the sole professional.

THE HUNTSMAN AND HIS HOUNDS

David Raley was Master and huntsman of the De La Brooke Foxhounds (MD) for six seasons before coming to Red Mountain as professional huntsman. He was also a practicing architect at the time. With no professional hunt staff and no one at the kennels during the day, Raley found the breeding, training, and hunting of De La Brooke's pack of American foxhounds to be a trying experience.

"I needed help," Raley recalled.

One day at a hound show he and his staff were waiting their turn

David Raley and his hounds do it their own way at Red Mountain. *Martin Engel photo*

in the pack class, nervously trying to maintain control of hounds. He looked out and experienced an epiphany.

"There was Todd Addis [then huntsman for the Marlborough (MD)]," he recalled, "totally relaxed, sitting under a tree—alone—with his Penn-Marydels all around him."

Raley saw the light. He built his Penn-Marydel pack mainly with drafts from Doc Addis, Marlborough, and Sandy Dunn at Kimberton. At the same time, he has maintained traces of superb American blood-lines from Piedmont, Orange County, and Middleburg in his Penn-Marydel brood bitches.

"Penn-Marydels have a place with the smaller clubs that have to get by with less help," he says. "They're just easier to deal with."

THE MELLOWING OF A HUNTSMAN

Like so many before him who became besotted by foxhounds, David Raley abandoned his architectural career to become a full-time

ROUGEMONT AND THE RED
MOUNTAIN HOUNDS

Red Mountain is named for the hilly, red clay terrain on the west side of the Flat River about twenty minutes north of Durham, North Carolina. It's a mostly wooded hunting country with trails maintained for good access through the hills and valleys and along the river.

Much of the late-nineteenth and early-twentieth-century architecture still stands in and around the town of Rougemont—wood-frame, clapboard-sided homes with prominent gables set into spreading roof lines atop broad porches in the southern tradition.

In the early twentieth century, Rougemont was renowned for quail and foxhunting. The Quail Roost Hunting Lodge was formed in 1875 by a group of Durham businessmen. One of the lodge members was John Sprunt Hill, great-grandfather-in-law of the current senior Master, Irmgard Hill. The club secured rights to hunt quail, dove, and turkey over three thousand acres of land, and in 1902 they formed the Quail Roost Shooting Club.

With the expansion of farming during the early 1920s, the area's quail population declined, and continued maintenance of the large quail hunting preserve was no longer feasible. John Sprunt Hill bought out the other members and in 1926 bequeathed the property to his son, George Watts Hill.

professional huntsman. He lives with his beautiful wife, Christine, not fifty yards from the kennels.

"We're so grateful for Christine," jokes Joint-Master Bruce Dalton within Raley's hearing. "Before David met her he was a real pain. Now he's mellow. It's so much more pleasant for all of us."

David and Christine met at a Shakerag Hunt Ball. The Red

The new owner of what was then Quail Roost Farm took a serious interest in cattle farming, while his wife bred, raised, and trained horses—hunters, jumpers, and steeplechasers. By the 1940s the farm possessed one of the premier Guernsey herds in the world. A birthday party for the herd's foundation sire was covered by *Life* magazine.

In 1952, Watts Hill donated his handsome Colonial Revival home to the University of North Carolina to be used as a conference center, and about two thousand acres of land to North Carolina State University for use as a teaching forest. That land still comprises much of Red Mountain's hunting country. Watts Hill's son and daughter-in-law—John Sprunt Hill II and his wife, Irmgard—made the remainder of Quail Roost their home in 1969, soon establishing the Quail Roost Stables.

The Red Mountain Hounds, of which Irmgard Hill was a founding Master, was organized that same year—a split-off from the Triangle Hunt. Over the years Irmgard has served the MFHA in several capacities: Director of the Carolinas District, Chairman of the Hound and Puppy Show Committee, and President of the Foxhound Club of North America.

Irmgard's Joint-Masters are Dr. Bruce Dalton and Garrison "Garry" Riggs. Garry's wife, Carol, serves the hunt as Honorary Secretary and whipper-in.

Mountain contingent had hired a bus to take them to Atlanta and return them to Rougemont afterward. Christine, born and bred to city life, arrived at the ball late, just having returned home to Atlanta from London where she was living and working. When Raley saw her enter the room all was forgotten: hounds, traveling companions, return bus schedule, everything.

The relationship started with a scrap, however, as they found themselves bidding against each other in the silent auction for a seedy, moth-eaten stuffed coyote. They talked. They danced. When the bus was ready to depart for North Carolina, Raley was nowhere to be found. In fact, Christine and two of her friends had abducted him, then abandoned him in a hotel room where he awoke the next morning still in his evening clothes, alone but for the companionship of his disreputable coyote. To her credit, Christine had the grace to return and drive him to the airport so he could get home to his hounds. The pair were married six months later.

CONVERSATION WITH A HUNTSMAN

I asked Raley to talk about the hound traits most important to him as huntsman of the Red Mountain Hounds.

"Speaking as a huntsman of Penn-Marydels, because that's what I happen to have, nose and voice are always the two most important things," he replied. "It's what the breed's been bred for, it's what they're noted for, it's what you always go back to. It's what makes a Penn-Marydel a Penn-Marydel.

"I love taking hounds down to Moore County (NC). Jody [Murtagh, Moore County huntsman] and I will take out twenty couple and mix our packs together. Now, that's voice! But even that doesn't compare to Doc Addis's hounds, which are about the loudest things you have ever . . . ever heard. They'll just knock you over.

"But for a hunting hound I don't want to breed for one particular trait at the expense of all others. I need the whole package. I need them biddable, but I don't need them to follow me around all packed up tight. I don't like that, and Penn-Marydels don't like that. They're more free-ranging.

"But I want them to come when I call them. While hunting, I expect them to turn when I turn. When I tap my horn I expect them to look at me and see which way I'm going. Which they do.

"I don't want to need a bunch of whips riding herd on them. Professional whips who are around the hounds all the time are consistent in their commands. But for whips who can't spend all their time around the kennels, we need a hound that is more simply handled . . . easy to deal with. They have to be flexible and go with how we do things around here. The Penn-Marydel is a great low-maintenance hound."

I was curious about Raley's reference to the bigger voice of Doc Addis's hounds. A Penn-Marydel is a Penn-Marydel, right? They all have big voices. Why, I asked, were Addis's more so?

"I'll give you the serious answer first and then the not-so-serious answer," Raley replied. "Addis told me once that if you breed a deep-mouthed dog to a deep-mouthed bitch, ninety percent of your litter will have the same deep voices. If you breed a deep mouth to a lighter mouth, you'll probably get about half of them with a big voice. The key is to find a bitch with a big voice. Dogs usually have big voices anyway. Every bitch I have got from Doc has had a tremendous voice.

"Now the not-so-serious answer is that Doc is probably getting a bit hard of hearing! He's getting older. He tells me, 'My hounds just aren't as loud as they used to be. I've got to breed for more voice!' It's incredible. His just have a different sound—more so than mine, more so than Jody's, more so than anyone's.

"Doc's says his eyesight isn't what it used to be. So he went and bred to Andy Ford's white dog. He wanted more white so he could see hounds better. That's how he picked his outcross.

"You have to breed to suit the huntsman, as opposed to always breeding for country. We hunt in such varied country in such varied temperatures. I want to be able to take my hounds anywhere in the United States and have a pretty good chance of starting some game."

31

THE WADSWORTH DYNASTY

One Hundred and Thirty-Three Years of Foxhunting in the Genesee Valley

2009

While I very much enjoyed visiting and writing about some of the newer and lesser known hunts during my tenure as Covertside *editor, it was always a thrill to become acquainted with one of the long-established hunts that sit at the very foundation of foxhunting history in North America. The venerable Genesee Valley Hunt in New York State occupies such a position.*

When Major W. Austin Wadsworth, MFH of the Genesee Valley Hunt, was elected as the first president of the newly established MFHA in 1907, he was the logical choice. His statesmanship, his wit, and the level of sport he showed would have been sufficient to mark him as a leader, yet it was his democratic policy of all-inclusiveness that put an American stamp on this British-inspired sport.

Marion Thorne, Joint-Master and huntsman, slipped her handheld GPS from the case attached to her saddle, peered at the small screen for a few moments, then shook her head.

"We're doomed," she murmured with a wry smile.

Immense fields of unharvested corn surrounded us on all sides. We had been enjoying the fruits of a real "hound hunt" for the past forty-five minutes. Hounds had found in a cornfield, had diligently worked their way up on their fox, got it running, finally pushing it

nonstop from one cornfield to another with tremendous cry, across
the hayfields and through the coverts in between, but now the pack
was split. Three foxes had just been viewed crossing the road in both
directions, and the cry of hounds was now coming from nearly all
points of the compass. Too much of a good thing. We were cubhunting, in August, in shirtsleeves, and the young entry were getting their
education. There was nothing for Marion to do but put her horn to
her lips and start walking.

I had come to Geneseo in western New York State for two consecutive days of early-season hunting with the Genesee Valley Hunt. I was
in good company. More than a century earlier, Harry Worcester Smith,
Teddy Roosevelt, Henry Cabot Lodge, the Hitchcocks, and the Bel-
monts thought enough of the sport here to be frequent visitors as well.

For the first day's meet, my host Eric Myer had mounted me on
one of his field hunters, a bay Thoroughbred called Zach. Strange
horses in a strange country are always a question, but Zach gave me a
beautiful ride from the start. He had a lovely gallop, easily adjusted by
a light touch on his snaffle mouth, and he carried me safely and
smoothly over the few panels that confronted us in that Haverford
Meet country. I had the pleasure of riding up with Marion and with
Martha Wadsworth, MFH, the former huntsman, which gave me the
opportunity to watch this wonderful pack of Crossbreds work. There
is no Field Master at Genesee Valley, and those who want to stay with
hounds do so by putting their horses into high gear.

A DISTINGUISHED HISTORY

There is no other hunt in North America with a more distinguished
foxhunting history than the Genesee Valley Hunt—four generations
of Masters and huntsmen from a single family, a founder of the Masters
of Foxhounds Association, two presidents of that association, and an
enviable record of conservation. With such familial continuity, the
hunt more nearly resembles Ireland's famed Scarteen, where hounds
have been owned and bred by the Ryan family for over three hundred
years, than it does any other hunt on the American continent.

Marion Thorne is the fourth generation of the Wadsworth Family to serve the Genesee Valley Hunt as Joint-Master and huntsman. With no Field Master here, the followers are the author; former huntsman Martha Wadsworth, MFH; and the field. *Bill Gamble photo*

When, in February 1907, Major W. Austin Wadsworth met with Harry Worcester Smith and four other Masters at the Waldorf-Astoria in New York to discuss the creation of the Masters of Foxhounds Association, the Genesee Valley (of which he owned forty thousand acres) had long been the center of organized foxhunting in North America. At the association's first official meeting later that year, Major Wadsworth was elected president.

The Major had established his hunt in 1876, the one hundredth anniversary of the Revolutionary War. Out of respect to his great-uncle Jeremiah, who served on General Washington's staff, The Major proclaimed that red coats would not be worn in his field. Hunt livery at the Genesee Valley specifies Colonial blue coats with buff collars for that very reason.

Major Wadsworth's home at the time of the hunt's founding was the Homestead, which venue provides the fixture for Opening Meet to this day. The Homestead remains the Wadsworth family seat and is today home to the present senior Master, W. Austin Wadsworth.

An architecturally complex structure, the Homestead has grown over the years from a small log fort built in 1800 to a stately home that has entertained legions of hunting guests from the famous to the not-so-famous. Much of the interior furnishing is unchanged from what was there in the nineteenth century, including the chain mail armor hanging in the main staircase, mounted big game trophies, ancestral paintings, leather-bound books, and the assortment of swords, pistols, muskets, and flintlocks adorning the walls. It is a museum, yet still occupied and breathing.

Major Wadsworth's hunt began as a trencher-fed pack, with each field member bringing his own hounds at the appointed hour. Although The Major was the designated huntsman, the chaos and confusion produced by each field member encouraging and rating his own hounds led in just a few years to his decision to develop his own pack of Welsh-English crosses.

From earliest times, Major Wadsworth was sculpting a uniquely American twist on the sport of foxhunting. Though he ran his hunt and managed the country as befits a benevolent dictator, he fostered a culture of democratic inclusiveness that has remained a core tenet of the hunt's philosophy to this day.

"I would rather see a farmer's boy on a mule at a meet," he said, "than the most elaborate creation of a London tailor."

The 1881 membership roll lists thirteen male and fifteen female honorary members. Over the next thirty years, according to the hunt's website, over one hundred and fifty people of all ethnic, religious, and economic backgrounds were invited by the Master to be-come members of the hunt.

The Major also possessed a well-developed sense of humor, which he employed to great success in his writings. To him we credit the well-known "Foxhunter's Bible," many lines of which are treasured by the literate foxhunter. Here are just a few:

Of the Farmer:
You may think that the honest farmer deems it a privilege to leave his life of luxurious idleness and travel around half the night in the mud for horses that have got out . . . by your leaving his gates open. . . . You are mistaken. He doesn't.

Of the Master:
The MFH is a great and mystic personage to be lowly, meekly and rever-ently looked up to. . . . His ways are not as other men's ways, and his lan-guage and actions are not to be judged by their standards.

Of the Fox:
Don't "give tongue" on a woodchuck. It will cause you humiliation. There is a difference in the tails.

Of the Hounds:
Keep away from them at all times and at every time. Even if you con-sider them worthless, the Master may be quaintly indifferent to your opinions. . . .

(The entire text of Major Wadsworth's "Bible" has been published in many books on foxhunting and also may be found on the hunt's web-site, www.geneseevalleyhunt.org.)

Recognizing that many of the young bloods in his field wanted nothing more than the opportunity to run and jump, The Major or-ganized the occasional drag hunt for their satisfaction. In the final paragraph of the proposed notice of the drag hunt to his followers we find yet another example of his understanding wit:

Some very swift hounds have been secured, and this drag will be laid as strong as possible, so that it is sincerely hoped the gentlemen racing with each other will not be annoyed by these stupid animals. Should they prove

to be a nuisance, however, the stupid brutes will be dispensed with altogether and the line flagged.

David Gray, the first author to popularize American foxhunting
stories, was a regular follower of Major Wadsworth's hounds, and
many of the stories published in his acclaimed *Gallops I* and *Gallops II*
volumes were based on actual events that occurred in the Genesee
Valley field.

When Major Wadsworth died in 1918, his son William P. Wadsworth was but eleven years old—too young to assume the responsibilities of MFH. For a little over a decade the Mastership of the hunt
was held by three other gentlemen, one of them a Wadsworth, until
1933, when William P. pronounced himself ready to take over the
office and the horn.

A highly regarded Master and huntsman with sixteen years as an
officer in the MFHA, William P. Wadsworth was a happy choice for
association president in 1970. He also authored the classic booklet,
Riding to Hounds in North America, which has provided advice and in-
struction on attire and etiquette, as well as sound hunting information
to countless newcomers to the sport. The booklet is still in print and
is available from the MFHA.

William P.'s son W. Austin and daughter Martha preserved the
family continuity by whipping-in and by, each in their turn, taking the
Mastership and the horn. W. Austin's stepdaughter, Marion Thorne,
who in her turn whipped-in to both Austin and Martha, represents
the fourth generation to have accepted the Mastership and carried
the horn. Marion's husband, Travis Thorne, whips-in to Marion.

A VARIED HUNTING COUNTRY

Geneseo lies approximately at the intersection of a line drawn easterly
from Buffalo (on Lake Erie) and a line drawn southerly from Rochester
(on Lake Ontario). The Genesee Valley is bisected by the Genesee
River, which runs northerly into Lake Ontario.

The hunting country is varied. There are areas of long, rolling hills partly cleared and partly wooded—green swaths of cropland cut out of large wooded coverts. There are flat areas of flood plain planted in cash crops of corn, soybeans, and alfalfa, also separated by large patches of woodland.

Then there are the "gullies"—another hunting world entirely—gouged out by the glaciers in wandering fingers with steep ridges, stone-faced cliffs, and running stream beds. The gullies are trappy and demanding, and the local horses get very fit following hounds down, up, and over the ridges.

THE HUNTSMAN AND HER HOUNDS

Marion Thorne began whipping-in to her stepfather, W. Austin Wadsworth, in 1982 and later whipped-in to his sister, Martha Wadsworth, after the horn was passed to her. In 2001, Marion succeeded Martha as huntsman and has been in charge of the breeding program as well.

Austin had whipped-in to his father, William P., but when he became huntsman he moved away from the English hounds in favor of Crossbreds. Many of the coverts in the country are enormous, and he wanted hounds that hunted themselves and were easy to rate.

"Austin did an awesome job," said Marion. "He really concentrated on nose and cry. He kept some of his father's English lines and in the late 1970s and early 1980s went to Brandywine to breed to a couple of American dog hounds there. One of them was Brandywine Bard. He must have had a great voice because that cry is still in the line.

"He went to Midland around that time," continued Marion, "and bred to Warcry, Warrior, and Watchman. Austin's program worked really well, and the hunting was great."

Austin bred very few hounds each year, because he was loath to cull his hounds, and just as the bloodlines were getting a bit close, the needed outcrosses fell into his lap. He inherited a local farmer's pack—eleven couple—consisting of all Midland breeding.

"He had Midland Nautical and Midland Dawson, who were great sires," said Marion. "Everybody used them—Ben [Hardaway], Randy [Waterman], others. There were bitches, too, that we used. It was really a boon for us, and all those bloodlines are still in our pack.

"Another boon was getting a lot of Piedmont hounds—about ten couple of unentered hounds—after Randy moved to Montana. They were a similar type to our hounds and seemed to nick well with the lines we had. They're excellent for my style of hunting and for our country. They're Crossbreds, but very American in type—more independent in their hunting style and suitable in the heavily wooded country, and easy to train.

"I also went to Warrenton when Jim Atkins was there and bred to a couple of his hounds. I got a bitch from him—a Potomac bitch—that was related to all those nice J-hounds that Larry [Pitts] has. We got a great bottom line going from her. They're smart, busy, and athletic. We've had to build the kennel fences higher and higher. They'll not only jump out but they'll release the latches as well!

"Jim Atkins gave me some great advice when I was starting out. He said, 'If you're working really hard to get a hound to do what you want it to do, you're just wasting your time. Cull it. There are plenty of other hounds in the pack.'"

Indeed, Marion finds there are jobs for hounds that don't hunt well in the pack. She has a good relationship with the gun dog people and night hunters in the Valley, and these individuals are happy to acquire well-trained hounds that don't run deer.

RIDING THE GULLIES

My second day of hunting was a kennel meet, and I got a taste of what hunting in the gullies was like. Although I thought with pride that I handled them creditably, I was assured later by the natives that the country hunted this day was strictly in the category of pre-novice compared to the *real* gullies!

I rode one of Marion's hunters—a big, bay three-quarter-bred called KC, in recognition of Kansas City from whence he came. He was also called The Cadillac, an apt alias. He had a long, easy stride and met every coop perfectly.

The meets in late August are scheduled for 6:30 a.m. Not only was the morning still dim, but it was exceedingly foggy. I assumed Marion would wait until the fog lifted before moving off, but she had no such thoughts. Then I recalled the cry I had heard from this pack on the previous day and realized that she didn't *need* to see hounds; she would surely hear them.

Once again I rode up just behind Marion and enjoyed watching the hounds. They are active, always working, and go right along in front of their huntsman. We had scarcely left the kennel when they found with a roar, and we were off. This fox must have been surprised in his bed for he was hard pressed from the start. We galloped through the dim woods, heard hounds approaching, and in the gloom ahead saw the dark shape of a wet, muddy fox shoot across the trail as fast as I've ever seen a fox move. Not two seconds later the hounds raced across, the entire pack in a frenzy of excitement, each throwing his voice in exultation, declaring his determination, right down to the last hound in the line. This fox never had time to work the gullies and cliffs in an attempt to elude hounds. After a fast burst of just ten minutes he very sensibly went to ground.

Marion dismounted, praised her hounds at the earth, and moved on. Within five minutes another fox was found. This one quickly abandoned the high ground, and I found myself descending rapidly at the gallop along twisting and turning trails, some with precipitous, vertical drop-offs to the side, over patches of deep mud, scrambling over loose stones, and splashing across the stream beds. Before moving off, Travis had cautioned me to keep up with Marion or risk being lost, and since I can still get lost in the woods near my own house, I was determined not to be left behind.

Marion is uncanny in her ability to stay with hounds in full cry. She has complete knowledge of the country and how the foxes run through it. The air was damp and heavy, there had been a shower the day before, and scenting conditions were excellent. Hounds never stopped running or speaking.

Unable to shake off its pursuers in the gullies, the fox took us back to the high ground and set his mask southward. We had good galloping over hayfields, through woods, over an in-and-out set of coops across the gravel road and into another large woodland, briefly in the open, back into the woods by the river, all the while in touch with the screaming pack. The pack swung easterly, and soon the radio crackled.

"Hounds have crossed the road and are in Eric Myer's yard."

There wasn't much good country remaining in that direction, and with horses' sides heaving, Marion decided to stop hounds. We had run nonstop for forty-five minutes on the second fox of the day, and no one could have asked for better sport from any pack.

After a superb breakfast laid on by Martha Wadsworth and assurances from the members that I had not yet experienced the *real* gullies, for which experience I would have to make a return trip, I set my own mask for home with a deep reverence for the sense of place, community, and continuity that this hunt embodies.

The fourth generation of Wadsworths have committed themselves to preserving what was handed down to them by their forebears. While Marion Thorne maintains the hounds and the hunting standards, other members of that generation apply themselves to the preservation of their country. Martha Wadsworth's nephew Eric Grace serves as executive director of the Genesee Valley Conservancy, with hunt subscribers making up over sixty percent of its board of directors. The Hunt and the Conservancy have been so successful in their efforts that they were jointly recognized at the 2008 Annual Meeting of the MFHA with the presentation of the Hunting Habitat Conservation Award.

32

FARMINGTON HUNT SHOWS SPORT, PEAK FOLIAGE, AND HOSPITALITY

2009

With this final hunting report that appeared in my last issue as editor of Covertside, I mark the close of a most satisfying and joyful chapter in my hunting life.

Pardon me, if you will, for paraphrasing here what I wrote in my introduction. This sport of foxhunting that you love offers never-ending opportunities to learn, discover, and increase your hunting pleasure. Pay attention to what hounds are doing. Read good books (see the suggested reading list). There is so much more to know!

Late October in the foothills of the Blue Ridge Mountains near Charlottesville, Virginia. The autumn foliage had burst into color practically overnight. The woods were aglow in the yellow, orange, and russet tones of the hardwood maples and oaks that populated the hillsides. Hounds were drawing ahead of us, and the only sounds were the muted footfalls of our horses on the rain-softened rides. Tony Leahy turned in his saddle.

"It's like a cathedral, isn't it?" he said quietly.

The MFHA directors and a few lucky others were guests of the Farmington Hunt Club, hosts this year of the annual fall meeting of association officers and directors. Farmington members graciously held back, allowing the guests to follow Field Master Ken Chapman and get a view of hounds working.

A deep-voiced hound opened, alone, but confident. Presently another joined in, then another, and one by one, the others affirmed that he had indeed found a fox they could hunt. The cry swelled as they trailed up on the line, and the horses lightened their stride across the grass.

With early morning temperatures suddenly in the seventies after a couple of weeks of cool weather, hounds struggled in the abruptly changed conditions. They worked well for huntsman Daron Beeney, however, and pushed their fox on through the woods.

The terrain at Farmington is more than rolling; it's hilly, but not mountainous. We crossed over ridges, climbing and descending, and forded streams in the low places. Anxious to stay in touch with hounds, we suddenly found ourselves precisely where the huntsman would rather have not seen us. Hold hard. The good news was the field got a chance to see some nice hound work.

We turned to see hounds come over the ridge and work their way down the hill in our direction, feathering sterns and speaking to the line. *We had clearly overrun the line.* Hounds came to our trail, checked, and tried back. *We had clearly foiled the line.*

I've heard said that the sign of a good huntsman is when his pack gets it right without his help. After trying back to no avail, hounds cast themselves forward on their own, picked up the line on the other side of the trail, spoke triumphantly, and ran on.

In the open, we ran across beautifully manicured hayfields that I would have been proud to call lawn. Late morning sun broke through, igniting the autumn hues on the wood line as the black rain clouds retreated behind the glowing trees.

The temperature rose, scent evaporated, and Beeney drew every stick pile in desperation, hounds trying all the while. They marked a fox at home in one of the stick piles but couldn't push him out.

Later, I commented to Beeney on the wonderful cry of his pack.

Farmington huntsman Daron Beeney inherited a mixed pack of American foxhounds of the old Bywaters breeding and Crossbreds of the Live Oak Hounds breeding. He likes the Bywaters–Live Oak crosses for his wooded country. *Evelyn C. Cowles photo*

"Yes, it's great for the field to hear, and good cry like that really pulls the pack together and improves the hunting," Beeney observed.

Daron Beeney came to Farmington directly from hunt service in England. He was huntsman to the Eglinton there and had previously hunted hounds for the Surrey Union.

At Farmington, Beeney inherited a pack consisting of twenty percent American hounds of the old Bywaters breeding and Crossbreds drafted by the Live Oak Hounds to the late Jill Summers, MFH. A long and powerful bond of friendship existed between Jill and Daphne Wood, and one can be certain that the Live Oak drafts were good ones!

Beeney found the Crossbreds to better suit his hilly and wooded country, and he continued Jill Summers's program, breeding the Bywaters bloodlines to the Live Oak Crossbreds.

"We don't have enough open country for the faster American hounds," he surprised me by saying. "Others might disagree, but that's my opinion."

He keeps twenty-five couple of entered hounds in kennel, and hunts a mixed pack. In addition to the Crossbreds, Beeney has one American hound from the Orange County, one English hound, and some Penn-Marydel crosses.

Our day with the Farmington hounds ended at sunset, at the hunt's clubhouse perched high on a hill behind the kennels. A south-facing veranda runs the length of the clubhouse, the view from which makes it obvious why Thomas Jefferson chose the heights of nearby Monticello for his own home. To the south, the moon waxed bright in its first quarter; a nearby mountain glowed in all its glorious color to the southeast; and between the two, a green valley stretched before us to the distant mountains. Welcome to Virginia, said Farmington Masters Carol Easter, Patrick Butterfield, and Joy Crompton.

CHAPTER SOURCES

2. *CLASSIC* magazine, February/March 1978

3. *The Chronicle of the Horse*, September 19, 1986

4. *Covertside*, July 1998; *Baily's Hunting Directory*, 1998/1999

5. *Covertside*, September 1998; *Baily's Hunting Directory*, 1999/2000

6. *Covertside*, March 2000

7. *Covertside*, July 2000

8. *Hunting and Country Illustrated* (UK), September 2002

9. *Covertside*, September 2001; *Baily's Hunting Directory*, 2002/2003

10. *Covertside*, September 2002

11. *Covertside*, December 2002

12. *Covertside*, December 2002

13. *Hunting and Country Illustrated* (UK), June 2002

14. *Covertside*, December 2003

15. *Covertside*, December 2003

16. *Covertside*, December 2004

17. *Covertside*, December 2004

18. *Covertside*, July 2005

19. *Covertside*, September 2005

20. *Covertside*, December 2005

21. *Covertside*, December 2005

22. *Covertside*, March 2006

23. *Covertside*, September 2006

24. *Covertside*, July 2006, March 2007, December 2007

25. *Covertside*, December 2007

26. *Covertside*, December 2007

27. *Covertside*, March 2008

28. *Covertside*, Summer 2008

29. *Covertside*, Winter 2008

30. *Covertside*, Summer 2009

31. *Covertside*, Winter 2009

32. *Covertside*, Winter 2009

SUGGESTED READING

INSTRUCTION AND INFORMATION

Foxhunting: How to Watch and Listen by Hugh Robards, 2006
   Each chapter takes the reader on the same hunt over the same country from the points of view of each of the participants: huntsman, whipper-in, Field Master, hounds, and fox.

Foxhunting in North America by Alexander Mackay-Smith, 1985
   A comprehensive guide to foxhunting in the United States and Canada.

The American Foxhound: 1747–1967 by Alexander Mackay-Smith, 1968
   The bible for every breeder and student of the American foxhound.

Gone Away by Mason Houghland, 1949
   A charming, beautifully written guide to all aspects of foxhunting.

Hounds and Hunting Through the Ages by Joseph B. Thomas, 1928
   The first comprehensive book on hunting with hounds written by an American.

Riding to Hounds in North America by William P. Wadsworth
   Small booklet containing sound hunting information and advice on attire and etiquette; available from the MFHA and *The Chronicle of the Horse.*

Thoughts on Hunting by Peter Beckford, 1781
    The bible of foxhunting; the first "how-to" book ever published on the subject; still relevant.

PURE ENTERTAINMENT

The Voice of Bugle Ann by MacKinlay Kantor, 1935
    A small novel about a Missouri night hunter and his hound by a Pulitzer Prize–winning American author.

The Daughter of Bugle Ann by MacKinlay Kantor, 1953
    The sequel to the first.

The Silver Horn by Gordon Grand, 1932
    A collection of some of the author's best-loved stories.

Some Experiences of an Irish R.M. by Somerville and Ross, 1899
    The most thoroughly hilarious and entertaining book about foxhunting ever written.

Further Experiences of an Irish R.M. by Somerville and Ross
    More of the same.

Mr. Carteret by David Gray, 1899
    After numerous readings, I still cannot read the title story without breaking into uncontrollable laughter.

AUTHOR'S NOTE

This short list of suggested reading will surely and justifiably be criticized for omitting countless excellent, humorous, informative, and entertaining favorites. My only defense is that a longer comprehensive reading list might be intimidating, and I firmly believe that readers who delve into any of these will quickly find their own way to other wonderful titles.

INDEX